The Limits of Health Reform

THE LIMITS
OF HEALTH
REFORM

The Search for Realism

ELI GINZBERG

Basic Books, Inc., Publishers

NEW YORK

Library of Congress Cataloging in Publication Data

Ginzberg, Eli, 1911–
    The limits of health reform.

    Bibliography: p. 215
    Includes index.
    1.   Medical policy—United States.
    2.   Medical care—United States.   I.   Title.
    RA395.A3G49   362.1'0973   77-75244
    ISBN: 0-465-04117-5

To

The memory of my mentor and friend,
Major General Raymond W. Bliss, M.C.

Who gave me the opportunity to
learn firsthand about the
potentials and the limits of health reform

Contents

Part Three

Prospects for Reform

Acknowledgments

THE RESEARCH in health policy from which the present work evolved has been assisted by grants, starting in 1973, from the Robert Wood Johnson Foundation. The analysis also draws on our ongoing research in human resources and manpower, including health manpower, which has received long-term support from the Office of Research and Development, Employment and Training Administration, U.S. Department of Labor. I am deeply grateful for this continuing support.

Miriam Ostow of the Conservation staff has greatly contributed to this effort by helping me to sharpen my views and by her extended work on the manuscript.

Ruth S. Ginzberg made time to review the manuscript and in the process contributed to its readability.

My friend Professor Rashi Fein of Harvard University permitted me to impose on him to read the manuscript; as a result it has been considerably improved.

Martin Kessler proved, once again, that what every writer needs is a good editor.

Sylvia Leef turned my yellow sheets into readable copy with great efficiency and good humor.

ELI GINZBERG

Conservation of Human Resources
Columbia University
April, 1977

Part One

Framework

1

Introduction

IN OUR society, it is still the citizens who, through their voice
in the marketplace and in the legislature, ultimately determine
how their money will be allocated. By deciding to devote 8.6
percent of its earnings to the health care industry—an industry
that employs one out of twenty members of the work force
—the American public has thus clearly indicated the importance it attaches to that industry's output.

This book does not pick up the challenge of the anti-es-
tablishment group, which contends that ever larger expenditures on health care will not buy freedom from disability or
significantly extend an individual's life. Rather it has a
narrower focus: to lead the reader through the processes of attempted health reform during the past three decades in an effort to deepen his understanding of what we ventured, where
we succeeded, where we failed, and why. When we have
learned about the recent past, we should be in a better position
to formulate realistic goals for improving our health care system and to avoid unduly high expectations that can lead only
to frustration.

In our review of this record, we shall not limit ourselves to the expanding health care industry but shall also explore that industry's place within the fabric of American society. Our basic political, social, and economic institutions present opportunities for constructive changes in the health care system, although they constrain the rate at which these opportunities can be pursued. We shall not consider desirable health reforms without also considering their costs in terms of commitments, resources, and controls.

This book, then, will focus on the possibilities of health care reform given the realities of contemporary American society. It will assume a continuity in the society's commitments to a federal system of government, a pluralistic economy, and the freedom of the individual to pursue his preferences with respect to residence, work, and the spending of his income.

The reader is entitled to an explanation of why such a large and complex subject as health care reform is dealt with so briefly, with a minimum of documentation, especially since the dominant style in the United States is to deal with weighty subjects in a weighty manner. Studies of a major political era, a major war, a dominant figure seldom comprise less than 500 pages; many are double that length, with additional pages of documentation. But there is more than one way to deal with a weighty subject.[1] And my preference is to select a few subjects, to distill their essence, and to place each subject in its broader social context.

This tract, then, addresses a basic question: What have we Americans been seeking to accomplish through our various social interventions, primarily governmental actions, directed toward modifying the structure and functioning of our health care system, and what judgment can be reached about their effectiveness?

First, let us differentiate this work from the conventional

approaches of social scientists who have studied the health care system. Recently, economists have questioned whether the large increases in total resources deployed in the health arena since the mid-1960s have resulted in worthwhile gains to the consumer through either increased longevity or reduced morbidity.[2] The economists' stock in trade is to suggest how the improved use of resources can result in more desired outputs. Unable to find unequivocal evidence of increased longevity and/or the reduction and elimination of disease, their concern has increased. Some have even suggested that the nation is in the grip of a medical monopoly that continues to extract more and more dollars from the vulnerable consumer-citizen in return for few additional useful services. Sociologists and political scientists, on the other hand, have initiated ambitious inquiries into the structure and functioning of the principal health care institutions, including the impacts of strong interest groups on the functioning of the system. Some of the best social scientists who study the health arena build on analytical models by organizing large bodies of empirical data to test various relationships, such as the determinants of hospital costs, the shifting balance in the supply and demand of various types of health manpower, and the estimated net costs that taxpayers in different income brackets would have to pay if national health insurance were introduced.

The present study, eclectic in approach, is focused on the process of health care reform. It relies heavily on the use of historical, institutional, and, on occasion, comparative materials to illuminate the play of those forces that can be mobilized in favor of reform and those that often coalesce to block or derail reform.

For many years, the American people have sought to make their health care delivery system more responsive to their needs, and it is likely that these efforts may accelerate in the years ahead. Thus, the Carter Administration has made a commitment to introduce some form of national health insurance. And the results of a recent Roper survey indicated that the public believes that despite the nation's rapidly expanding outlays for health care, it should further increase them.[3]

Most members of the American Medical Association and many laymen believe that the reform of the health care system is the province of physicians, who have the knowledge and expertise to assess alternative policies and solutions. Others, remembering Talleyrand's comment that war is too serious a matter to be left to the generals, believe that issues of health reform are too critical to be left to the medical profession. But the issue is moot. Since government—federal, state, and local—is now the source of more than two of every five dollars expended for health care, the control and reform of the health care industry is, and will certainly remain, in the political arena. An advanced technological society such as the United States can no longer rely exclusively on the private sector to provide the goods and services, including health care, that it needs, wants, and can afford.

The linkage that now ties health care to politics supports our focus on the processes of health reform. Much of the recent action toward health care reform has taken place in the political arena (Medicare); Congress has recently enacted legislation aimed at a relocation of physicians to underserved areas (Health Professions Educational Assistance Act, 1976); and the likely future confrontation over national health insurance will also take place in Congress.

Before we can consider the theme of health reform, we must decide how to treat it. Clearly, there is no one answer. The subject invites an extended historical treatment in which the major reforms of the past quarter or half century, both those proposed as well as those enacted, are reviewed in depth

to illuminate the forces that determined the different outcomes. A full treatment would have to include not only reforms in the governmental arena, such as Medicare, but also
reforms in the private and nonprofit sectors, such as the shift
among physicians from general practice to specialization and
the large-scale growth of the Blue Cross Plans.

The present effort seeks to illuminate the premises on which
reform measures were based, the innovations proposed to accomplish the stipulated goals, the extent to which the changes
were successful, and an explanation of the failures.

When some analysts uncover deficiencies in the health care
system, they are quick to formulate suggestions for remedying
them, without sufficiently considering the political realities
that are likely to block action. Politicians, for example, seek to
avoid difficult and contentious issues. The politicians' stock in
trade is to estimate the numbers who favor and the numbers
who oppose a specific line of action, but they do more than
take a simple head count. They also take into account that
those who can lose from a proposed change are more likely to
organize to thwart it than the larger number who might gain
from the change but who are less engaged in the issue or the
outcome.

This simple principle of political life helps to explain much
that otherwise would be incomprehensible, such as the persistence of two parallel systems of hospital care in New York City
despite four decades of repeated caveats from blue ribbon commissions and committees that such duplication is costly to the
taxpayer and dysfunctional for the poor and the medically indigent. The explanation is that no mayor has seen sufficient
political profit in confronting the leadership of the voluntary
hospital system, which, so far, has preferred to leave the municipal hospital system in place. Every mayor has known that
substantial gains would result from the consolidation or

merger of these two systems or from the dissolution of the municipal system, but no mayor could afford to do battle with the economic, social, and religious establishments that control the voluntary hospital system and exercise a controlling voice in the city's life.

We cannot, however, equate repeated failures in health reform with the venality of politicians. Responsibility also belongs to the faulty diagnoses of analysts who frequently err in assessing the malfunctioning of the system. Other failures are the result of remedies that do not adequately address the primary difficulties. For instance, in 1946 the federal government initiated a hospital construction program designed to provide facilities for underserved areas, particularly rural communities. But what the legislators did not consider was how these communities would be able to attract and retain the health professionals that they would need in order to make effective use of the new facilities once the hospitals were built.

Another cause of slippage between reforms and accomplishments is the exaggerated claims of the proponents of change. Some years ago the leaders of the psychiatric profession in New York City badgered the governor to provide financing for clinics, citing the fact that the city had a shortage of outpatient facilities for the mentally ill. They attempted to buttress their case by pointing out that additional clinics would help to prevent mental illness, would slow the inflow of patients into the state hospital system, and would result in a reduction in total expenditures for mental illness. All three of these contentions were dramatic, but they were also unsupported by the facts.

The misplaced enthusiasm of many reformers resulted in similarly exaggerated claims for a variety of reforms and innovations such as prepaid group practice, community health clinics, home care for chronic patients, and other sensible and desirable changes. Each of these changes holds some promise of improving health care, but no one of them, not even all of them together, would necessarily alter significantly the health care available to the American people.

A final lesson from the past four decades is the prevalence of widespread misconceptions about the potential of government, particularly the federal government, to accomplish whatever it sets out to do once it is willing to spend large sums of money. The reality is different. Even an energized and committed citizenry is seldom able to maintain an adequate level of funding for any purpose for any length of time. Consider the events following the transient euphoria that accompanied the passage of Medicare and Medicaid. Within two years, both the federal and state governments cut back on each program, first by eliminating the 2 percent override in reimbursing hospitals under Medicare, and second by tightening eligibility requirements under Medicaid.

The limits to what government can accomplish go beyond the number of dollars that it is able to appropriate. Ours is a representative democracy; those elected must remain sensitive to the values, goals, interests, and fears of critical groups that helped to elect them and that can, if sufficiently disturbed, defeat them at the next election. The scope for governmental initiative on any issue is always limited by the changing forces in the political arena.

This interpretive study is directed primarily to exploring the processes of health reform in the U.S. since World War II in order to distill important lessons from that experience for the politician, the health professional, and the public as they continue to search for ways of strengthening the delivery of health care services to the American people.

2

Problems and Policies

ONE OF the important works of twentieth-century economics was written in 1923 by John Maynard Keynes. His *Tract on Monetary Reform* was an attempt to alert legislators and others in decision-making positions to the fact that World War I had permanently altered the role of gold in international economic relations.[4] If Great Britain and the other Western nations continued to shape their policies in accordance with the rules of the international gold standard, Keynes stated, their economies would run slack and their unemployment rates would inevitably rise. An appraisal of the economic changes wrought by the war, he said, was essential for sound economic policy.

What we can learn from Keynes is the importance of confronting reality and determining whether existing theory can help to illuminate it. In the event that the prevailing theory is found wanting, our task is to explore new lines of inquiry, more in consonance with the changing reality.

The present work focuses on the potentials for health reform and reviews the efforts at health reform that have engaged the

American people in recent decades with an aim of extracting useful lessons. Even if a nation understands its history, it may fail in the pursuit of its goals. But without understanding, it is crippled.

First, let us acknowledge that wide differences exist among the electorate about the urgency of pressing for major reforms in the health care system. Some believe that the country is at least four decades late in adopting a system of national health insurance.[5] They argue that if President Roosevelt had taken the lead in 1935, when the Social Security legislation was being drafted, some form of national health insurance would have been introduced at that time. But then as now, both the leadership and the electorate were divided among the proponents of national health insurance, the opponents, and the considerable numbers in between who were not yet ready to adopt a strong position for or against the reform.

So the debate continues. Some proponents of national health insurance argue that since almost every other modern industrialized country has included health care within its system of social insurance, the United States should do likewise. These proponents feel that since our social legislation currently offers protection against other contingencies—for example, loss of income, permanent disability, old age, and death—it should expand its scope to include health insurance. And they have allies among those who doubt that low income groups will ever have adequate access to health services unless our society "socializes" the costs of such care. Still others are convinced that the current "nonsystem," as they refer to the production and distribution of health care services, cannot be rationalized until a national system of financing medical care is established.

Among those who oppose such comprehensive reforms are many who have examined the social insurance systems of the

West European nations and are less impressed with their experience in the delivery of health services; they see no reason for the United States to follow the same path. Some of the antagonists believe that the shortcomings of our present health care system can be remedied without the disturbances that would accompany major reforms by providing coverage for those not now covered or covered inadequately by private insurance or governmental programs. Still others, cognizant of the tremendous increases in total health care expenditures during the past decade, question whether any reforms in financing are the answer. They see the challenge of overcoming shortcomings in the quantity and quality of the services available as involving more than an alteration in the methods of payment.

Disagreements about how to finance health care represent one area of controversy; a second centers around the production and distribution of trained manpower, particularly physicians. Shortly after World War II the Magnuson Commission (1952), one of the first of many groups of advisers to the President and the Congress, proposed that the federal government assume specific responsibility for part, if not all, of the costs of educating physicians and other types of health manpower.[6] A quarter of a century and several billion dollars later, Congress discovered that many aspects of the manpower problem were still unresolved. We will note a few that continue to command attention.

Substantial increases in the total supply of physicians raised the ratio of physicians per 100,000 persons from 135 in 1950 to 174 in 1974, or by about 24 percent in twenty-four years.[7] The corresponding increase in the ratio of nurses per 100,000 persons was steeper, from 201 in 1949 to 407 in 1974, or by 102 percent.[8] But as the Congress and the public learned with difficulty, increases in the total supply do not assure that communities and groups that earlier encountered difficulties in obtaining access to health providers will be able to see a physician more easily. The spill-over theory so attractive to economists, who believe that market forces will lure professionals from areas with excessive numbers to areas of relative scarcity, does not work in the short run and may not work even in the long run. Most of the states that had a low ratio of physicians or nurses to population in 1950 have a low ratio a quarter century later—even after the total supply has increased substantially.

A second unresolved manpower issue concerns the appropriate balance between specialists and family practitioners. During the past decade, an increasing number of professionals and laymen have argued that American medicine is overspecialized, that we have too many specialists and too few primary-care physicians. Many of these critics recommend an even division between generalists and specialists but they are unable to explain the basis for this recommendation. Moreover, they ignore the difficulties of classifying physicians in one or the other category or of accounting for the fact that many specialists do in fact engage in primary care, such as an orthopedist who tries to help an elderly arthritic patient. Despite these unresolved issues, Congress, in its Health Professions Educational Assistance Act of 1976, mandated that we achieve a 50:50 ratio in residency training by 1980 and indicated that it would intervene further if the desired outcome were not achieved.

Another only partially resolved manpower problem, addressed in the same legislation but modified by subsequent administrative action, involves a new policy toward physicians who are graduates of foreign medical schools (FMGs). For a series of complex reasons—a desire to assure residency opportunities for the larger number of prospective graduates from American medical schools, concern over the quality of training that many FMGs have received, dissatisfaction among patients treated by physicians who do not speak English—Congress has acted to reduce radically the flow of FMGs into the United States. However, the early implementation of the legislation has been postponed because many hospitals, particularly in the eastern part of the United States, depend on FMGs for their house staff and would be unable to operate without them.

Prior to the passage of Medicare and Medicaid in 1965, many analysts believed that our health care system would be swamped by persons who previously had not sought treatment because of lack of financial means. Experience proved these fears exaggerated. For the most part, physicians, clinics, hospitals, and nursing homes were able to handle the increased demand for services, sometimes immediately, more often after a relatively short time during which new institutions (especially nursing homes) were opened and old ones expanded. However, the lack of comprehensive benefits, particularly for long-term care, under Medicare for persons sixty-five and older and the restrictions governing eligibility of low-income families under Medicaid—as well as the restrictions on the benefits to which the eligible population is entitled—help to explain why, in 1977, the issue of access to medical care remains a major concern. Millions of individuals and families do not have adequate private health insurance and do not qualify for medical benefits under either governmental program. They must either pay for the medical care they receive, rely on relatives or philanthropy, or use up their savings and assets so that finally they become eligible for governmental assistance.

The problems of access and financing are closely linked. For the elderly poor one of the disappointments following the passage of Medicaid was the extent to which both the federal and state governments decided because of financial stringencies to cut back the range of services they provide. In recent years, despite fast-rising Medicare expenditures, the federal government's contribution to the total health care expenditures for the elderly has declined.

This brief review suggests continuing difficulties in financing medical care: existing insurance plans and government programs do not include payment for various types of care; millions of individuals and families have no insurance coverage and are not eligible for governmental assistance; third-party payors, both private and governmental, are under pressure to slow the rise in their expenditures, which constrains their ability to improve coverage.

In considering reform measures we must distinguish between a new system of national health insurance, which would address the problems of persons not now covered or inadequately covered under private insurance or existing governmental programs, and the additional resources, financial and other, that would be required to assure comprehensive benefits for everyone.

The issue of the quality of medical care, in varying guises, has been on the nation's agenda since the end of World War II. The first major thrust at improving the quality of medical care was the strong effort to improve the state mental hospitals. These had earned the soubriquet "snake pits" because so many of their patients were half-starved, physically mistreated, without therapy, and condemned to inactivity. If the rate of spending by state legislatures for the care of the mentally ill is used as the measure of reform, then the educational and missionary zeal of psychiatric and lay leaders and of voluntary mental health associations has paid off. Certainly, the coming of age of drug therapy and the more enlightened attitude of the public toward the mentally ill contributed to improving the quality of care. However, this favorable assessment must be read against the abysmal conditions existing at the end of World War II; it must not be interpreted to mean that institutionalized and released mental patients receive acceptable treatment today. The claim put forth here is more modest: that the quality of care received by mental patients has improved considerably over the last quarter century.

Since physicians tend to protect one another against charges by outsiders, no study has ever been able to assess the frequency with which general practitioners and specialists provide deficient care or the seriousness of the consequences that result from their errors. During the last decade, however, the marked increase in malpractice suits has turned the spotlight on professional work of such demonstrably poor quality that juries and judges have granted extraordinary damages. But the heart of the issue of quality has less to do with demonstrably bad judgments and actions by the occasional provider than with raising the level of care characteristic of the lower half of the spectrum of physicians.

It is always difficult to define quality. Competent physicians disagree, often strongly, about preferred therapy. Even when they agree, they often differ in their assessments of the patient and his environment or of the correct therapeutic approach. Since there are significant regional and cultural preferences in medical treatment, since the question of financial resources must be factored into the therapeutic equation—a millionaire can spend $50,000 a year for the hospital care of a schizophrenic child, while a family with a modest income obviously cannot—since the patient must not be placed at risk without his or his family's consent, we see that a simple question of quality is anything but simple.

When, therefore, Congress decided in 1972 to legislate medical quality by stipulating that physicians in each geographic area form Professional Standards Review Organizations (PSROs) to assess the treatment plans and discharge goals for their Medicare and Medicaid patients, it was more a testimonial to the legislators' faith in law than to their knowledge of medical practice. It should be added that members of Congress must have had second thoughts about this new program, since they have moved slowly to appropriate the necessary funds to implement it. We must further note that the PSRO legislation was directed more to controlling the federal government's reimbursement costs to hospitals than to improving the quality of care that patients receive.

Difficult as the concept of quality is, it cannot be dismissed. We cannot consider access to medical care without considering quality, just as we cannot ignore considerations of cost when we consider the issue of quality.

Considerations of the costs of health care are becoming more prominent in the national debate, although many reformers prefer to disregard such a mundane issue when human life and suffering are involved. One need only look at recent expenditure trends to understand this growing concern. Total outlays for health increased from $39 billion in 1965 to $139 billion in 1976; on a per capita basis, expenditures increased from $198 to $638.[9] Although some reformers might like to disregard the money issue and focus on the substantive problems of improving the system of health care delivery, those who must argue around a collective bargaining table or vote in the legislature are increasingly seeking ways of slowing the rapid rise in expenditures for medical care.

The urgency of cost containment has led several states such as Connecticut and Maryland toward radical experimentation. They have moved to a system of cost control for hospitals similar to that followed by commissions with power to control the prices and profits of public utilities. But it is not clear that this approach will prove practical in the hospital field, with its many relatively small units, diverse patient loads, and other idiosyncratic factors—such as the amount of endowments, the age and condition of plant and equipment, and the nature of the neighborhood.

Because of the difficulties inherent in government regulation and the limitations of relying on the market, many analysts look to national health insurance as the only certain way to bring about successful cost containment. They expect to achieve such cost containment through economies which will follow the elimination of competing organizations that sell insurance, economies in the administrative mechanism that will oversee the new system, and economies that will encourage provider groups to furnish comprehensive prepaid care. These prepaid plans will cover all of the health needs of the enrolled population, at a fixed cost per person. It is expected that under such a plan incentive contracts will be made with provider groups to encourage them to explore more efficient ways of delivering health services and that experiments will be made with forward budgeting that sets a ceiling on expenditures for the year.

Although we cannot know in advance whether these putative gains are realizable, the recent record of the growth of governmental bureaucracies, the market strength of physicians, the entrepreneurial barriers to developing prepaid health plans, and the difficulties attendant upon negotiating with the federal government all justify caution.

Even an abbreviated list of major issues on the nation's health agenda would include the matter of equity, which has been defined as the establishment of a single level of care for all persons, irrespective of their poverty or wealth. The protagonists of this approach correctly contend that in an affluent society like ours it is unconscionable that a poor man cannot obtain life-extending or life-protecting health services.

When the most important therapeutic agents, from antibiotics to aspirin, are priced within the reach of most people, when rich and poor alike are admitted to a hospital in emergencies, when most children receive their inoculations free or at a cost that does not strain the family's budget, our society will have moved a fair distance toward equity in health care. The critical issue is the definition of "fair."

Let us, for the moment, distinguish between an acceptable level of care for all and the same level of care for all. The latter cannot be achieved; the former can, with time and effort, be approximated. A single standard of care for all is chimerical because it is a fact that in all societies characterized by marked differences in income, power, and influence among its people, those who are closer to the top of the hierarchy, defined by either wealth or political clout, are better able to obtain access to the desirable parts of the health care system—the most capable physicians, the best equipped and maintained hospitals, the most advanced forms of therapy. There are substantial differences in every other service sector—in education, recreation, transportation, housing—for the same reason that they exist in health. The differences reflect the limited pool of available human and physical resources, and, as a consequence, those with more wealth or influence can command the better services.

Since health care often transcends diagnosis and therapy and is affected by a wide range of conditions and circumstances, such as the availability of food, housing, household help, and unearned income, it must be clear that equity in health care is little more than a slogan. The distribution of health care services in communist and socialist countries does not reflect a single level of care. Political leaders have better access, higher quality of treatment, and more propitious outcomes. Still, the thrust toward equity is important both because of the human values it seeks to realize and because it offers a test for realism in health reform. To ignore the pressures for equity would be as unrealistic as to promise that it will shortly be achieved.

This book addresses each of the major issues that have been identified in this chapter—access, quality, cost, and equity. It postulates, as we have indicated, that the current debate over health reform requires, first, more understanding about how the health care system has operated and operates today and, second, an understanding of the values and structures that characterize our American democracy. Since our health care system has undergone marked expansion during the post-World War II period, there are lessons to be learned from our earlier efforts at health reform, both in terms of goals that were formulated but not pursued because a consensus could not be achieved and in terms of the objectives that gained widespread approval and were pursued with varying degrees of success. We cannot ignore this rich record of effort, accomplishment, and failure.

In attempting to extract the lessons of our recent past, we will proceed as follows. The next chapter provides an overview of what we have attempted since World War II, the problems we encountered as we altered our system of health care, and the results we achieved, as well as the costs we incurred.

The last chapter in Part One considers some of the difficulties in planning for improved health care in a society that relies on the competitive market to attract and distribute resources and to price its products. As the chapter seeks to make clear, it is not easy to meld these two approaches: one looks to the market for guidance and the other relies on "planning" by nonprofit and governmental instrumentalities. Chapter 4 also addresses the pulling and hauling that has characterized the evolving health care system; this antagonism is a result of the confrontation between the providers, who want to maintain maximum freedom to pursue their goals, and the consumers, communities, and governments, whose interests often conflict with those of the providers.

Part Two addresses the most critical and contentious issues in the arena of health reform. First, how can we enable underserved groups to obtain broadened access to health care? Second, since medical intervention may occasionally have no positive outcome and may even have deleterious results, we will focus on considerations of quality and the actions that can be taken to improve the average level of health care provided the American people. Chapter 6 also suggests that broadened access often does not mean improved quality, since each goal makes a demand on scarce resources.

The third chapter in Part Two explores the possible actions we can take to moderate the rapid rise in health expenditures. This issue is frequently formulated in terms of what the American people can afford to spend on health, but a better formulation would posit that increasing the proportion of the nation's income devoted to health may not be justified by the benefits that accrue to the public.

The last chapter in Part Two considers the issue of equity. The discussion goes beyond the question of a single standard of care for all groups; it considers equity among persons of different ages, different levels of education, different group affiliations, different disabilities. We suggest here the unlikelihood that any society will ever provide equal health care for all classes of its citizenry, in every age group, in every region, whatever their disabilities. We see that the quest for equity becomes a moving target.

Part Three seeks to encapsulate the lessons extracted from a review of the nation's recent efforts to broaden access, improve quality, contain costs, and pursue equity in health care. Considering these lessons, Chapter 9 juxtaposes the ambitious

goals that many health reformers advocate with the realities
that set limits on the ways in which the health care system
operates. Health reform has been hobbled by the lack of understanding of two points: the health care system cannot be significantly modified by any single change, even one as sweeping as national health insurance; and the reforms in health
care must be broadly congruent with the existing value structure of a democratic society. There are limits to using legislative and administrative mechanisms to specify what small or
large institutions, from the neighborhood drugstore to a major
teaching hospital, are or are not permitted to do.

Since we will have become aware of the constraints on
health reform, the penultimate chapter offers a limited
number of targets which if achieved would result in improved
health services.

The final chapter presents an overview of the process of
health reform in a democracy and a forecast of the future
when we must seek an intermediate goal, somewhere between
modifying the health care system so that it can be more responsive to the needs of the citizenry and not jeopardizing the
values and institutions that give meaning and direction to our
society. The thrust of this chapter, as of the book, is to increase
understanding in order to improve policy.

3

The Postwar Experience

A COMMON WEAKNESS of advanced nations, particularly one that like the United States has enjoyed such rapid economic and technological development, is to be so concerned with its present problems and future prospects that it neglects to study its history and therefore misinterprets its past. As we have seen, one manifestation of this bias is the widely accepted presumption that only small improvements in our health care system have been made in recent decades because we still have not enacted a system of national health insurance, a system of organizing and financing health care that is now the accepted pattern in most advanced industrial nations. However, if we consider the totality of the system, including the way in which Americans now pay for health care, we see that our health care system has undergone many significant changes at every level—in the production, financing, and delivery of medical care.

In this chapter, we will identify the principal transformations that have taken place, we will put them into historical context, and we will pinpoint the unresolved issues that are of major concern to the nation. Although most of the changes that we will discuss have taken place since World War II, their roots go considerably farther back.

Most calls for social reform and most of the answers to them involve money. Therefore, this account of the important transformation in the U.S. health care system will consider how the nation has dealt with the question of national health insurance; the new departures in the financing of hospital care and physician services that accompanied the growth of Blue Cross and commercial insurance; the much enlarged role of the federal government in financing biomedical research, in expanding the supply of health resources, and in covering a significant part of the costs of the health care of the elderly and the poor. Each of these themes warrants attention.

As early as 1912, a small number of leaders concerned with social insurance and health issues concluded that if the middle class and the poor were to have access to good medical care, this country needed to enact a system of health insurance under governmental aegis, a view that the American Medical Association supported for a period of years.[5] But it was not until the publication in the early 1930s of the final report of the prestigious Committee on the Costs of Medical Care, established by eight foundations with broad medical and lay membership, that the issue of financing health care received national attention.[10]

This distinguished committee, after a series of incisive studies on many aspects of the health care system, was divided in its recommendations to the American people: a minority of the committee members recommended a national system of health care based on prepayment and strong governmental leadership to integrate the several levels of care from initial points of patient contact with physicians and community hospitals to large specialized treatment centers. The other members were divided between the conservatively inclined, who opposed any major reforms, and the liberals, who advocated a large number of specific reforms but stopped short of joining their more radical colleagues in advocating a national system of prepayment. The deepening depression eventually shifted attention away from health to basic economic reforms.

The issue of national health insurance surfaced again when the Social Security Act was drafted in the mid-1930s, but President Roosevelt decided to omit health insurance from the new bill in order to increase its prospects of passing. The issue reemerged for a third time in 1939, when Senators Wagner and Murray and Representative Dingle introduced a bill that failed to pass. The next push came in the late 1940s, when President Truman threw his support behind a revised national health insurance bill; once again, the opposition, led by the American Medical Association, proved too strong.

One reason why Congress did not enact national health insurance at the end of the 1940s was the growth of voluntary and commercial insurance plans for hospital care, which included payments to physicians when patients were hospitalized. The Blue Cross Plans were started in the 1930s and their growth was accelerated during World War II, when the payment of premiums by employers was recognized by the War Labor Board as a fringe benefit that did not violate efforts at wage stabilization.

The long depression, which lasted throughout the 1930s and was followed by the elimination of civilian construction during the war years, also resulted in a substantial postwar deficit of hospital beds. This deficit was particularly acute in the underpopulated areas that had never been able to afford the large capital sums required to build a modern hospital. As a result, Congress passed the Hill-Burton Act in 1946, which allocated federal funds for hospital construction to communities judged to have a deficiency in acceptable hospital beds. This was the first of many federal efforts to enlarge the pool of health resources.

Another reform thrust, already touched on briefly in the last chapter, concerns the country's postwar efforts to reform its mental hospitals. This was a direct consequence of the war. Indeed, a large part of the stimulus for reform came from psychiatrists who had learned in the Armed Forces that mental patients treated early had the best chance of recovery and that most patients did not require hospitalization on locked wards. Upon their return to civilian life, they sought to apply these lessons. The war had other consequences for the health care system. Thus, the organization of the medical services of the Army and Navy contributed substantially to speeding the trend toward specialization of physicians in civilian life. The Armed Services assigned and ranked physicians according to whether they had passed their specialty boards.

Similarly the growing militancy of the nursing profession at the end of the war was stimulated by the enhanced status, prestige, and income that they had experienced on active duty in the Armed Forces. They were officers; for the most part, they served as managers, they seldom provided direct nursing to the sick and injured, and their pay and perquisites were considerably above what they had earned in civilian life. In general, the war provided a case illustration of the importance of allied health manpower and the critical role that paramedics, under proper supervision, could play in the delivery of preventive, therapeutic, and rehabilitative services. Medical corpsmen often had sole responsibility for providing care at medical units that were too small to justify the assignment of a physician.

Perhaps the most important, albeit indirect, influence of the war on the nation's health care system was its demonstrable effect on the 15 million who served in uniform. From initial screening to discharge, the soldier or sailor who required medical attention was likely to receive a level of treatment far superior to what he had known at home. Moreover, the service environment, with its emphasis on nutrition, prophylaxis, and preventive measures to avoid disease and injury, raised the level of health consciousness of these 15 million persons and their families. The most positive influence was the performance record of the combat medical units, which were able to save 96 out of every 100 battle casualties.

The war also showed those involved in health policy and the delivery of health services how organization could rationalize the use of health resources and improve the quality of care rendered, particularly through regionalization of care and the use of physician extenders. The basic reform of the Veterans Administration hospitals, which took place under Generals Bradley and Hawley in the late 1940s, and the new linkages established between VA hospitals and their neighboring medical schools were reforms that benefited both.

Having failed to get Congress to enact health insurance legislation, President Truman, toward the end of his administration, appointed a commission to report on alternative routes the federal government might follow to improve the nation's health care. The President's Commission on the Health Needs of the Nation (the Magnuson Commission) recommended that, since changing the financial base was not practical, the federal government increase the flow of resources into the health system via expanded investments for research, manpower, and facilities. Two pieces of legislation were in place: the Hill-Burton Act and the National Institutes of Health (the federal biomedical research structure). Under the leadership of the Democrats, Senator Hill in the Senate and Representative Fogarty in the House, and with major assistance from the NIH bureaucrats and the leaders of the academic medical community, Congress followed the Magnuson Commission's recommendations in the 1950s and early 1960s and steadily increased the flow of federal dollars into biomedical research and the expansion of hospital facilities.

Federal dollars for research, which annually approximated $1.3 billion by the mid-1960s, did more than broaden and deepen the research base.[11] They also helped to keep the medical schools financially afloat. In the early 1950s, the American Medical Association had balked at approving direct federal support for medical education but it was willing to tolerate support via the research route.[12] Neither the federal government nor the American Medical Association, and certainly not the public, understood the subsequent effects of this backdoor financing of the medical schools on their primary mission of preparing practitioners.

In time, many questionable, even dysfunctional, consequences of this large flow of federal monies for research were distinguishable. For instance, the standing of physicians shifted: that of the skillful clinician was down, that of the medical scientist in the laboratory was up. Deans of medical schools were unable to prevent a substantial erosion of their power to plan and lead, since principal investigators were able to attract funds on their own. The number of young physicians who extended their studies beyond internship and residency to include postgraduate training increased substantially, and this in turn reinforced the trend to more narrow specialization. The emphasis in medical education shifted even more toward the biological nature of disease; little attention was paid to the environmental settings in which people live and work.

The American Medical Association was opposed not only to direct federal subsidy for medical schools; until the mid-1960s, it also opposed any efforts by the federal government to expand the number of medical schools or their enrollments. The rate of expansion was also constrained by the AMA's insistence that a new school be carefully planned and adequately financed before it could secure accreditation under state or private auspices.

The next thrust in health reform efforts, which was characterized more by sparring than by action, started in the late 1950s and early 1960s. Despite the substantial, some might say phenomenal, growth of hospital insurance, the frustrated reformers pointed out, quite correctly, that a significant minority of the population had either no hospital insurance or such inadequate coverage that it would be bankrupt in the event of a medical catastrophe. An even more serious shortcoming in hospital insurance, they said, was the linkage between coverage and employment. When an individual lost, or retired from, his job, he was likely to lose his coverage. Most insurance carriers refused to permit retirees to convert from a group policy to individual coverage, or permitted it only at a prohibitive cost. As a consequence, most older persons had no hospital insurance precisely at the time of their lives when they most needed protection. Finally, the fact that most insurance policies covered only inpatient treatment led to serious dislocations by encouraging the overuse of expensive hospital facilities with associated cost escalation, to the neglect of ambulatory care.

A cynic might observe that commercial and community insurance plans would deservedly disappear if the U.S. were eventually to adopt a system of national health insurance that would leave no place for them, for insurance companies have repeatedly demonstrated a lack of initiative by failing to act when action was called for. Through the mid-1960s hospital insurance plans were deficient in two major regards: (1) a former worker was unable to convert his group policy to an individual policy and (2) most people required protection against major medical expenditures. The insurance industry moved so slowly to correct the first defect that the federal government had to step in by passing Medicare. With respect to the second, the industry did at long last respond when it recently pushed major medical coverage.

The slow progress of government action in this area is instructive.[13] During Eisenhower's second administration (1956–1960), hospital protection for the aged moved to the forefront of Congressional and public debate. The Democratic Party platform in 1960 contained a plank in favor of adding to the Social Security system, insurance covering hospital bills and other expensive services for the aged; John F. Kennedy adopted this plank as one of his chief legislative goals. Just prior to the election (1960), Congress responded with the passage of compromise legislation, the Kerr-Mills Act, which made limited funds available to the states to enable them to provide medical care to low-income aged persons. Although successive efforts were made throughout the early 1960s by the Kennedy Administration to pass a hospital insurance bill, it was not until 1965 that enactment was achieved. Then President Johnson secured passage of not only an expanded Medicare program including both mandatory hospital care and optional coverage for physician services, but also a last minute addition of Medicaid, a federal-state program aimed at improving access to the health care system for millions of indigent and certain categories of "medically indigent" persons.

Thus thirty-three years after the Commission on Financing the Costs of Medical Care first drew attention to shortcomings in the prevailing mechanisms for financing health care, Congress took action to assist the two groups most in need of special consideration—the aged and the poor. Not even the most enthusiastic believer in private insurance and the "free enterprise system" would any longer deny that these groups required governmental assistance. Even the American Medical Association, once it was assured that the new legislation would not be used to disturb existing relationships between physicians and their patients, capitulated. Congressmen had heard from their constituents. Too many older persons who had always been independent were being forced onto the welfare rolls because of a costly illness, their children brought to the brink of insolvency because their parents had inadequate health insurance.

Shortly before Medicare was passed, Congress also moved directly and aggressively to increase the pool of health manpower, and its efforts expanded in the late 1960s and early 1970s. It made funds available for construction of schools, for the relief of schools in financial distress, for expanded enrollments. These monies augmented the substantial indirect support of educational institutions by awarding research contracts and graduate training fellowships. The total annual federal support for health professional schools in Fiscal Year 1974 amounted to $1.7 billion, about one-third of which represented direct expenditures for health manpower expansion. [14] The output of physicians increased by half between the mid-1960s and 1970s.

By the early 1970s, the worst of the health resource deficits were out of the way: the bed shortage of the early post-World War II period was relieved and an oversupply of beds was increasingly noticeable in many parts of the country; research funding was at the $2 billion level, more than a tenfold increase in stable dollars from the level of the early 1950s; [11] there was a steadily increasing ratio of physicians, nurses, and allied health personnel per capita; and the most egregious problems in the financing of health care had been greatly eased by Medicare and Medicaid. Under these circumstances one might have assumed that the nation would now enter a period of relative stability in the health arena. But the facts tell us otherwise. Throughout the first half of the 1970s leaders in the health professions, in Congress, and among the consuming public insisted that there was serious trouble on the health front. At one point in 1969 President Nixon talked of a "crisis."

Despite, and perhaps because of, the tremendous increase in national expenditures for health—the federal government's contribution increased from about $5 billion to over $40 billion annually during the decade following 1965—discontent, alarm, and forebodings continued.[15] And the indictments were directed toward almost every aspect of the system.

First, despite the assumption of responsibility by both federal and state government for many millions of persons who previously had to go without medical care or rely on themselves, their families, or philanthropy to cover their medical costs, the critics justifiably claim that many people still have limited access to the system. The most disadvantaged groups include those who live in outlying areas with no physicians or health care facilities. But the largest numbers of the underserved are the inner-city poor, primarily minority group members, who are unable to find practitioners willing to treat them. In the mid-1970s, there was not one pediatrician in private practice in Harlem,[16] and the ratio of private practitioners to population in the Chicago ghetto was about 1 for 5,000 people.[17]

Those concerned with preventive and other health services for children are also disturbed by the evidence that more and more preschool youngsters are not receiving basic inoculations.[18] Many nursing home patients who need medical evaluation or treatment have not been seen by a physician in six months or a year. The health services available to migrant workers are generally rated below, often far below, an acceptable level. Although Medicaid, Medicare, and the expansion of subsidized neighborhood health centers and outreach programs for rural areas have markedly improved the access of previously underserved groups to medical care, many are still not being adequately linked to the health care system.

Unfortunately, the substantial increase of government funds to cover the health expenditures of the elderly and the poor had some untoward consequences. As we have noted, many planners had feared that the new entitlements would swamp the existing resources, but this did not happen. What did occur was a steep acceleration in the unit and total costs of care.

In retrospect, it is clear that the large additional sums flowing into the system dissolved many of the established barriers against spending. Hospitals acquired new equipment, added expensive new services, agreed to pay their house staffs living wages, established a weaker defense against the wage and salary demands of their allied health and service workers, and otherwise increased their outlays substantially. They did all this knowing full well that their expenses would be reimbursed by third-party payors; that is, by insurance companies or the government. The increasing numbers of people who were insured not only for hospital care but also for other forms of health expenditures further lowered the bars against indiscriminate spending.

In the past, physicians had often provided care to the poor at a reduced charge or at no charge. Those who served in clinics and who treated patients on the wards were traditionally reimbursed not in money but in privileges and prestige—the right to admit private patients to hospitals and to teach. Today, the federal government pays for all services that physicians render to Medicare patients in and out of the hospital. One might conclude that the government often pays twice for the same service: salary for the house staff is part of the hospital's expenses that are included in establishing its reimbursement rate, and the supervisory physician's salary is often billed and reimbursed separately, although much of the care that Medicare patients receive is given by the house staff.

The increase in funds flowing into the health care system helped to pay for many services that previously had been contributed. Most important, the new payment mechanisms, especially those used to reimburse hospitals for all proper expenses, removed most of the preexistent barriers to cost containment. The rise in hospital and health costs in the decade since the introduction of Medicare and Medicaid has been a deep and growing cause for concern. The Carter Administration, as the Nixon Administration in the period of wage-price controls, felt under sufficient pressure to undertake special efforts to cap these costs.

The source of the concern has multiple roots. Some believe that a disproportionate amount of the nation's disposable income is directed to health care—approximately one out of every eleven dollars. Since many Americans eat poorly, live in inadequate dwellings, have little or no savings, and are able to enjoy only the most modest recreational activities, the dollars that they must spend on health care leave fewer for them to spend on other important items.

Another reason for concern about the steeply rising costs of health care is the burden that it places on those who must cover ever larger premiums for various forms of health insurance. Since the self-employed and many employed workers pay part or all of their premiums themselves, those in the low income brackets are under increasing strain to meet the payments. Even when employers pay all of these premiums, the money eventually comes out of the working person's compensation. If the premium rate goes up, the employer takes this into account in estimating his next wage proposal.

The alternative to raising the premium rate so that it is commensurate with increases in hospital costs and professional fees is to reduce the care afforded the insured person. This is an alternative but not a solution. If the central aim of hospital insurance is to prevent financial hardship to the patient, then it is necessary to reduce the risk of larger out-of-pocket payments by the patient and his family. It may be possible to eliminate one or another extra from a policy without compromising its purpose, but it is a real danger that rapidly rising premiums will undermine the insurance system for large numbers of low income participants.

Many critics of the health care system believe that the cost escalation reflects inefficiency in the use of health resources. As examples, they cite the large amount of unused capacity, the imbalance between outpatient and inpatient capacity, and lax hospital administration, all of which result in overstaffing and low productivity, extended patient stays unjustified on medical grounds, and other forms of ineffective utilization.

In addition, many critics feel that the public is being "ripped off" by strategically situated providers—physicians who are often able to set their fees without competition, pharmaceutical companies that are able to price their products to obtain huge profits, and others who extract monopolistic returns. For example, many radiologists and pathologists have been able to work out highly lucrative arrangements, especially with community hospitals, whereby their contracts guarantee them a percentage of all billings by the hospital for work performed by their department. Since they alone are able to perform the work, they enjoy a monopoly position and their earnings exceed those of most other members of the hospital staff.

Some years ago, Dr. John Knowles, then the director of the

Massachusetts General Hospital, shocked the public by suggesting that the steep rise in hospital costs already underway at that time was only a precursor of things to come. He saw the possibility of hospital per diem costs of $300 to $500, a forecast that was given little credence at the time. In 1977 we know that a small number of major medical centers are already above the lower bound of Dr. Knowles' estimate and that more will exceed it within a year or two.

The fact that insurance plans have not yet been torpedoed by the repeated necessity to raise premiums does not mean that we can look to the future with equanimity. No one knows how long insurance plans will be able to raise their premium rates by 10 to 20 percent per annum, but it is inevitable that at some time, perhaps reasonably soon, they will begin to lose subscribers. If and when that happens, the health care industry will face a true crisis. The present system depends on most Americans being protected against large out-of-pocket expenses when they are hospitalized. If a significant minority of those now covered were to lose their insurance, new and dramatic changes in the health care system would become inevitable.

In addition to cost, several other factors have also conspired to focus the public's attention on the quality of the health care that it receives. First, there are the large awards made by juries in malpractice suits that are based on unequivocal evidence of demonstrated negligence on the part of physicians, hospitals, pharmaceutical companies, and other providers. The frequency of such suits and the considerable number of large awards that result cannot be explained primarily or solely in terms of hostile patients and avaricious lawyers. They attest to widespread inadequacies in the health care system.

Since quality involves the skill, competence, and conscientiousness of physicians and other members of the staff, the availability of resources, both institutional and individual, and the condition of the patient and the nature of his complaint, the scope for honest differences among competent professionals with respect to diagnosis and treatment is wide. Although it may be relatively easy to standardize procedures for routine interventions, the physician's major challenge is to be alert to deviations and to make allowances for what is idiosyncratic about the patient and his condition.

In the mid-1970s, the medical societies, state legislatures, and Congress took a number of initiatives on the issue of quality that sought among other things to contain the runaway costs of malpractice insurance, costs that for certain surgical specialties had reached more than $20,000 per annum for adequate coverage.

As of 1977, the problem of malpractice insurance seems to have peaked, and it no longer generates hysteria. However, the chief reason for the present lull is that physicians and hospitals have been able to pass on the higher premiums to consumers or third-party payors. Physician-sponsored insurance companies or state-supported agencies have stepped in to provide coverage when commercial underwriters have withdrawn. Many hospitals have initiated self-insurance, and some physicians also practice without insurance, protecting themselves by avoiding the most vulnerable procedures. There is scattered evidence in many states that both the number of medical malpractice lawsuits and the amounts awarded to the victims of malpractice have dropped, and as a result, insurance premiums are no longer rising as rapidly as they did in 1974 and 1975.[19] But if malpractice insurance premiums continue to rise at the currently restrained rate of 20 percent annually, (relative to the doubling and tripling of 1974–1975) difficulties are certain to arise should efforts to control physicians' fees be pursued aggressively.

And even though the malpractice issue has been momentarily contained, the level of quality provided by the health care industry remains a matter of concern. The 1972 amendments to the Social Security Act that established the Professional Standards Review Organizations (PSROs) are regarded as only a modest contribution to quality control. They may stimulate a group of physicians to more actively monitor the care given to patients in hospitals or even in the community at large, but since many medical societies continue to resist the placing of one more piece of apparatus between physician and patient, Congress has had second thoughts about the viability of this approach. As of early 1977, the score card with respect to PSROs reveals that they are making "cautious advances." Although no PSRO has yet been fully approved, 67 are in the planning stage and 105 have received conditional designation, which means that they are performing partial reviews in their area. It is now expected that by October 1978, which is the target date for full designations, only about 20 will be approved.[20] Although about one-half of all eligible physicians are currently members of a PSRO, there have been serious organizational difficulties in such important states as California, New York, New Jersey, and Michigan. Part of the organizational difficulties stems from professional conflicts; others reflect a lag in funding; still others reflect weak support from Washington.

However, the continuing efforts to improve the quality of health care in the educational and service areas, as distinct from the regulatory spheres, is laudable. The efforts extend from the diffusion of the best practices at the nation's teaching hospitals to the large array of continuing educational programs sponsored by the professional societies and medical schools.

Nevertheless, much more needs to be done in the area of quality assurance. What is unclear is whether primary reliance should be placed on educational procedures or on control mechanisms. Nor is it clear whether either one or both of these approaches will prove more than palliative, given the gaps between education and practice and between the forms and reality of control.

Much of the impetus for the transformations of the American health system, particularly the forces that led to the passage of Medicare and Medicaid in the mid-1960s and those now backing national health insurance, comes from our concern with issues of equity. For a long time, Americans have been bombarded with data showing that the poor, who presumably need more health care than the wealthy since illness and low income are positively associated, have long had less access to the system because of their inadequate financial resources. Recent data indicate that Medicare and Medicaid have gone far to narrow the gap in access, though not necessarily in quality, between individuals and families with high incomes and those with low incomes. With the outstanding exception of dental care, the rates of utilization of medical service are no longer conspicuously different for rich and poor.[21]

The first transformation in the post-World War II era was the success of voluntary hospital insurance, which benefitted the large middle class; this was supplemented in 1965 by governmental programs that provided basic coverage for the aged and the poor.

The second major development in the post-World War II years was the substantial governmental investment in enlarging the pool of health resources through expanding educational facilities and training and through supporting biomedical research.

A third and more subtle development involved the changing attitudes of the public toward health care. We have seen that World War II introduced an entire generation to a system of health care far superior to that which most of them had known in civilian life. This experience reinforced a desire for the better health care that was becoming available through science, technology, and communications.

Nevertheless, although the country may not be facing a crisis in 1977, it is uncertain about the performance of its health care system and about the reforms it should pursue to enable the system to be more responsive.

But in evaluating the equity of our health care system, more than equality of access is involved. Let us, for example, look at the *type* of care available to members of minority groups with low incomes in New York City—a metropolis with a large concentration of health resources. These New Yorkers receive most of their ambulatory care from a Medicaid mill or in the emergency rooms and outpatient departments of municipal or voluntary hospitals; when necessary, they are hospitalized, primarily in municipal hospitals. Now compare this with the health care available to a member of the upper middle class in the same city, who depends on a diplomate in internal medicine for routine care and who is referred by him to different specialists whenever his complaint points to the need for specialized attention; when necessary, this person is hospitalized in a private room in a large medical center. Clearly, any pretense to equity fades in the face of this contrast.

What about the future? As far as national health insurance is concerned, we see marked differences of opinion among strategic groups. The liberal-labor wing of the Democratic Party favors the introduction of a federalized system of national health insurance tied to an annual ceiling on budgetary outlays and containing strong incentives for the expansion of group practices based on capitation. The conservatives in both parties do not favor such an ambitious program of reform. They would prefer to reform Medicaid, particularly its administration, and to provide some additional protection against catastrophic illness for middle income families.

While waiting for the electorate to indicate whether it wants to tackle national health insurance or put it once again on the back burner, Congress finally succeeded in reaching agreement on another aspect of basic health reform involving physician manpower. After a prolonged stand-off because of differences between key committees in the House and Senate on the principles of effecting physician redistribution, a new health manpower act was passed in October 1976 (PL 94-484). The act makes future federal aid to medical schools dependent upon student commitments to practice in underserved areas upon the completion of their training. And, reflecting Congress' conviction that the nation faces an imbalance between primary-care physicians and specialists, it provides for continuing support of residency programs in family practice.

Congressional action on these two fronts reflected agreement among the legislators that some of the more serious deficiencies in access to health care could be overcome only by tying federal support to the distribution of physicians by region and specialty. Congress had concluded that its earlier actions, which had been directed primarily toward increasing the supply of health professionals, were inadequate to accomplish these broader objectives. But we must consider the prospect that a decade hence the defects to which Congress believed it was responsive in 1976 will not have been significantly ameliorated.

Since the introduction of Medicare and Medicaid in 1965, total federal expenditures for health care have increased approximately eight-fold, from around $5 billion to $40 billion annually in 1976, with no leveling off in sight.[15] This has occurred despite several approaches tried by Congress and the executive departments to halt the escalation. These efforts have included a variety of mechanisms aimed at cost containment, from eliminating the 2 percent override on reimbursable hospital costs in the original formula for Medicare and Medicaid payments to seeking the assistance of the Institute of Medicine of the National Academy of Sciences in establishing a revised and, it was hoped, less costly plan for paying for physicians' salaries in teaching hospitals. Without a detailed appraisal of all these approaches, which has not yet been undertaken, it would be irresponsible to conclude that they failed. Nevertheless, the steep and continuing increases in federal outlays for health care services suggest that to date, efforts directed at cost containment have had at best only a slight moderating influence. This explains why the Carter Administration is determined to explore new ways of capping federal outlays, at least limiting them to a specified amount of annual increase to which hospitals, the principal recipients of federal health dollars, would have to accommodate themselves.

The federal government would take the lead to limit the amount of increase, above the preceding year, in its reimbursement formula. Other third-party payors—state and local governments, Blue Cross, and commercial insurance companies—would follow suit. Hospitals would be on notice that if they spent more, they would have to cover the excess from other sources, a difficult if not impossible task.

Congress' concern with the performance of the health care system was evident in its passage late in 1974 of a comprehensive health planning act that encourages the states and the newly designated health service areas to consider their priority needs against available resources, and to develop plans that can lead to greater effectiveness and efficiency in the use of these resources in meeting the health needs of the population. A cynic might point out that, when action is difficult, planning offers an inexpensive substitute. Nevertheless, Congress did put the considerable prestige and some resources of the federal government behind this planning effort, which emphasizes the need for local initiatives to improve the functioning of the health care system. The planning act implicitly recognizes that, even with substantial federal assistance, little can be changed for the better until the leadership in each area determines what needs to be done and sets about taking the first steps to bring about the desired reforms.

Once again, considerable time must pass before expectations versus results can be weighed. It may be that the planning act of 1974 will turn out to be no more successful than earlier efforts at regional and comprehensive planning under federal stimulus. But whatever happens in the years ahead, the nation will be more sophisticated about the potentialities and limitations of local initiatives in the restructuring of the health care system. This lesson, together with the mounting body of evidence about federal initiatives, should strengthen future strategies for the reform of the health care industry.

This chapter has called attention to the major forces that have shaped and reshaped our health care system. In 1977, with the advantage of hindsight, we see a continuing unstable equilibrium between the minority of avid reformers who believe that significant progress waits upon a major overhaul of the financing and delivery of health services, and the majority who have recoiled from radical reforms but have sought to improve the system by increasing the available resources. In tandem with this disagreement, we see the growing recognition among many that structural reforms and additional resources, even together, may not close the gap between the public's expectations of access for all to an acceptable level of care and the limitations of effectively restructuring the health care system.

4

Market and Plan: Facing Both Ways

FOR MORE than four decades, conservatives and liberals have held divergent views about the merits of national health insurance, particularly about the ability of the market—the mainstay of the American economy—to produce and distribute adequate health care services. Protagonists of the market do not usually insist that we rely exclusively on the market to meet all of our health needs, just as opponents of the market do not insist that we place total reliance on governmental direction, here called "plan." But the two groups differ greatly with respect to both the causes of the present defects of the health care system and their remedies.

Thus, the market enthusiasts believe that most of the present difficulties, particularly those centered around escalation of costs, are the direct result of government intervention and of excessive reliance on powerful nonprofit institutions such as Blue Cross and the voluntary hospital system. They believe that only if market forces are given more play can we expect improvements. The other group believes that no modern health care system can operate efficiently if primary reliance is placed on the profit motive to attract resources and distribute services.

This chapter will not attempt to choose between market and plan; instead, it will review the evolution of our health care system during the past decades for the purpose of identifying the extent to which policy has relied on one, the other, or both, and the consequences that have flowed from these different emphases.

First let us describe what the two terms, "market" and "plan," mean in relation to the delivery of health care services. By "market," we mean the pressure on entrepreneurs in an industry to make a profit, to obtain and use resources efficiently and thus to be able to price their product or service below that of their competitors; the search by consumers for sellers who offer them the most for the least; the bankruptcy and subsequent withdrawal from the industry of entrepreneurs whose costs remain consistently above those of their competitors.

In addition, "market" implies such a large number of competing entrepreneurs that they cannot get together to agree on common practices, such as wage offers or prices. It also implies consumers, seeking to get the most for their dollars and spending their money carefully so as to gain the greatest possible satisfaction from their limited means.

In the health care arena these conditions, implicit in a functioning competitive market, are indeed largely absent. Although some private hospitals have experienced a modest expansion in recent years, most hospitals are operated by government or by nonprofit organizations that together account for over 90 percent of all bed capacity. This pattern was established long ago. The most distinguished hospitals on the East Coast, some of which go back to the colonial period, were started and have continued as nonprofit institutions; the local elite would assume the responsibility for raising capital funds and covering operating deficits with an occasional assist from state government. Private hospitals have always been suspected of being money-making mills that shirk their communal responsibility to treat the poor or educate the new generation of physicians. Moreover, quite irrespective of the entrepreneurial form, the concept of multiple establishments competing for the citizen's dollars by offering superior services at the lowest possible price has little relevance for hospital care. Even large cities have only relatively few hospitals, and those are located in different neighborhoods. Local residents tend to use local hospitals. With the improvement in urban transportation, many now seek hospital care out of their neighborhoods, but not without incurring extra costs in terms of time and transportation.

The relatively small number of hospitals in urban centers means that their administrators are able to meet and to agree upon policies, especially labor policies, which account for about three-fifths of their total expenditures. Hospital administrators try not to compete with each other in such a way as to drive up the wages and salaries of nurses or other personnel. Nor, in the opinion of some analysts, do consumers shop for hospital care; unless there is an emergency, most people follow the recommendations of their physicians about when and where to seek admission to a hospital. Thus the use of the market model, which would see consumers shopping for hospital care in the same manner as they shop for refrigerators or automobiles, is irrelevant.

We have considered the market first in terms of hospital

care because hospital care represents the single largest component of health care expenditures. It is about twice the size of the next item, physicians' services, which together with hospital care account for about two-thirds of total health care expenditures. How useful, then, is the market model in explaining the behavior of individuals and families in obtaining physicians' services?

In any community with more than one physician, consumers have some choice in deciding which doctor should treat them, and, in turn, the physician has some control over the selection of his patients. But implicit in a well-functioning market are, first, some knowledge on the part of consumers about the service they are purchasing and, second, the absence of collusion on the part of producers over the prices they set. Clearly, these conditions are not present in the market for physicians' services. Unless a physician has a grossly unsatisfactory record, the consumer is hard-pressed to distinguish the more skilled from the less skilled. True, the physician's qualifications, his formal training, and his hospital affiliations provide some guidance. But even if the consumer attempted to inform himself thoroughly, he would soon realize that as a layman with inadequate information he must choose among professionals whose training and experience he cannot judge.

Until recently, medical societies prohibited their members from advertising, and it is established practice that physicians do not reveal their colleagues' mistakes of judgment or action to the public. Moreover, physicians in the same location have frequently followed a pattern for setting fees that moderates, if it does not eliminate, price competition among them.

If we consider briefly the remainder of the health care industry—the one-third of total expenditures represented by outlays for dental care, pharmaceuticals, supplies and equipment, nursing home care—we find that, although much of the output is produced by private, profit-seeking enterprises, this sector of the market cannot be deemed competitive. For many of the drugs and much of the specialized equipment there are no effective substitutes. The suppliers often sell a product that they have developed in their own research and development laboratories, and until others in the industry are able to catch up with them, they are likely to enjoy a quasi-monopolistic advantage. Moreover, physicians rely on the products of certain companies in the belief that the quality of their products is superior to that of competitors. Let us add, however, that physicians reach this conclusion more often on the basis of the advertising and marketing pressures to which they have been exposed than on objective knowledge.

In light of all this, it is difficult to see how the model of the competitive market can be used to explain the economics of the health care industry. One need not contend that competition is totally absent; it clearly is not. But it is sufficiently restricted and confined to argue against acting on the assumption that an intensification of competition can provide a realistic solution to the industry's problems.

Let us now turn to what is incorporated in the term "plan." How much of what is produced and distributed in the health care industry falls outside of the model of the competitive market and reflects potent nonmarket forces, such as the direct participation of government and nonprofit institutions and mechanisms?

Again, let us take hospitals first. For most of the nation's history, capital available for community hospital construction was the result of philanthropic efforts, primarily from wealthy lay leaders and, to a lesser degree, from religious groups. In recent decades, the role of philanthropy has diminished as hospitals have tapped alternative sources of funding, largely by borrowing from the money market and from state and federal agencies (assuring payback through interest and depreciation charges allowed by third-party reimbursement).

Although there is some competition at work in these capital transactions—underwriters must assess the financial worthiness of the prospective borrower, and the hospital that seeks funds will attempt to obtain them under the most favorable conditions—the hub of the transaction lies in the payback mechanism, which, as we have seen, is linked to the hospital reimbursement system, which, in turn, depends primarily on the actions of government and of the nonprofit Blue Cross Plans.

Historically, the pricing of hospital care has had little in common with the pricing of services in a competitive market. And since the passage of Medicare and Medicaid in the mid-1960s, hospitals have been reimbursed by third parties for over 90 percent of their costs incurred in providing care, including interest payments on money borrowed for capital extensions and improvements. Under these circumstances, there has been only limited pressure on the trustees and the administrators to control costs. Pressed by the professional staff to stay in the forefront of medical advances, and pressed by the nursing and service staffs for higher wages and improved fringe benefits, the hospital leadership has had little incentive to fight either group. A fight could result in lowered staff morale, which in turn is likely to be reflected in patient dissatisfaction and a loss of institutional status and prestige. It was much easier for the hospital leadership to go along with the higher costs.

Our country has never relied on the market to provide hospital care for the poor; that has been the task of philanthropy and government from the beginning of colonial settlement. Since World War II, new instrumentalities, primarily nonprofit and commercial insurance, have been created that serve as intermediaries between the consumers and the providers of hospital care. The shift from market to plan was further accelerated when the federal government began to provide important tax benefits to employers who pay for much of their employees' hospital insurance. Those who pay for their own health care insurance and medical services also are entitled to tax benefits. Finally, the federal government today pays for most of the hospital care for the elderly and shares with the states the cost of the care of the poor. If "market" requires the direct involvement of the consumer in determining what he buys, how much he buys, and from whom he buys, we must conclude that the market model does not describe the hospital care industry in the United States today.

With respect to the second largest component in the health care complex, physician services, the shift from market to plan has also continued during the past three decades, although at a slower pace than hospitalization. Federal and state governments pay for most of the physicians' services for Medicare and Medicaid patients. And the rapid growth of Blue Shield and major medical insurance, together with the growth of prepayment plans, has reduced the proportion of direct consumer payments for physicians' services from 66 percent in 1960 to 39 percent in 1975.

For dental care, drugs, appliances, and nursing home care, the displacement of the market has been slower though still perceptible. In the early 1970s, insurance for dental care finally got underway, and by the end of 1975 about 35 million persons had some form of dental expense protection, up threefold from only five years earlier.[22] Drugs and appliances were still bought largely by the consumer on the open market, although hospital insurance covered most drugs used by inpatients.

Government via Medicaid and welfare played a major role in the fast growing nursing care industry. In 1976 about half of all nursing home care was covered by government reimbursements. If current regulations requiring that Medicare patients be hospitalized for at least three days before they become eligible for nursing home care were modified or removed—on the theory that the federal government would thereby save money since some patients could be treated in less costly facilities—the proportion of all nursing home care covered by government would probably rise even more rapidly.

This schematic account underscores that, whatever justification there may have been for using the market model to describe the health care industry prior to World War II, governmental and nonprofit institutions have increasingly dominated the industry during the last quarter century. This move from market to plan has not been fully understood either by the public or by its political and economic leaders. And for good reasons. The pressure to reduce the risk of financial catastrophe to the middle class in the event of serious illness was the principal reason for the growth of hospital insurance. There was also pressure to assure reasonable access to health services for the poor and elderly. These two principal social pressures moved the United States away from reliance on the market.

However, the steep escalation of the costs for health care in recent years serves as a warning that the removal of market discipline can have ominous consequences. That is why, in the last few years, many in decision-making roles have begun to seek ways to restructure the health care system to rely more on the market. At the same time, federal and state governments have moved towards increasing regulation and control over various sectors of the industry that earlier had been left alone. The paradox of seeking both more market and more plan is nowhere better illustrated than in the Kennedy-Corman plan for a federal system of health insurance. The plan would legislate a massive increase in the powers of the federal government to plan, finance, and control the health care industry while at the same time it aims to generate heightened competition among providers, especially physicians who would be encouraged to join prepayment groups and compete for patients under incentive-type capitation contracts.

Comprehensive national health insurance is still in the planning stages and it remains to be seen whether it will materialize. In any case, it may be useful to consider the differences between the protagonists of the market and those of the plan, and their policies aimed at improving the quantity and quality of benefits while seeking to restrict cost escalation.

The following case illustrations present, first, efforts directed at enhancing the role of the market and, second, efforts aimed at strengthening the mechanisms of social intervention. In both instances, the illustrations involve critical components of the health care industry—hospital care, physicians' services, and drugs and appliances.

Consider, for example, the enthusiasm with which the Nixon Administration in 1970 decided to support Dr. Paul Ellwood's proposal to encourage the growth of Health Maintenance Organizations (HMOs), a new term for prepaid group practice based on annual capitation payment, because of their presumed capacity to provide comprehensive health services to the American people at a lower cost than the prevailing system of fee-for-service plus hospital insurance.[23] Basing his arguments on experience garnered in Minneapolis-St. Paul, a community with a high proportion of hospitalization insurance and a low percentage of minorities, Ellwood advocated that the federal government facilitate the growth of prepaid plans by overriding state legislation that impeded the formation of such groups and by making funds available for their initial development.

However, as the election of 1972 approached, President Nixon lost most of his enthusiasm for the idea, partly because of the mounting opposition of organized medicine. Nonetheless, Congress acted favorably on Ellwood's proposal in 1973, but, as happens frequently in the legislature, the act that emerged was so hobbled by amendments that a new HMO would find it difficult and expensive to compete with the alternative arrangements already available. Both preexistent and new plans were discouraged from applying for designation as HMOs. To remedy this situation, Congress passed the Health Maintenance Organization Amendments of 1976 (PL 94-460), which modified requirements regarding the scope of benefits and open enrollment in the hope that a greater number of organizations might qualify for funding.

In any case, the capacity of HMOs to bring about a major improvement in the quality and cost of American health care remains under dispute. Prepayment plans have continued to grow, but slowly. Nor has the willingness of several large private insurance companies to put venture capital into the development of prepayment plans assured their success. Thus an experienced company, Connecticut General Life Insurance, sponsored a Brooklyn HMO that fell so far short of its enrollment target that it had to shut down within three years. A recent insightful article in the *New England Journal of Medicine* that reviewed the experience of an HMO in the new city of Columbia, Maryland, sponsored by Johns Hopkins, discusses a long list of problems including the difficulties of establishing and maintaining a congruence of interests among enrollees, physicians, and local hospitals.[24] The Harvard plan, after a difficult start, appears to be over the hump.

Few HMOs that serve a high proportion of Medicaid patients, who are heavy users of health services, have been successful. Moreover, given reasonable alternatives, many middle class patients find unattractive a system that restricts, frequently severely, their choice of physicians. And most physicians are not eager to join a prepayment plan because they foresee the difficulties of converting the plan for an HMO into a satisfactorily operating health service organization.

One additional point: It is somewhat incongruous that proponents of the market approach should press for HMOs, which require a governmental subsidy to become operational. There are few analogies in the private enterprise sector of potential competitors requiring the assistance of government to start up. The essence of a market economy is the attraction of new resources, human and capital, into a sector that offers prospective profits. Even the most avid supporters of HMOs have not contended that the health care industry offers such an incentive. The obverse is closer to the fact: even with a subsidy, it is hard to develop a new entrepreneurial structure for health care.

A second approach aimed at increasing competitive forces specifically in the most expensive and escalating area of health costs, the reimbursement of hospitals, has been to experiment with incentive reimbursement formulae that seek to encourage the expansion of low-cost hospitals at the expense of high-cost facilities. This may well turn out to be a worthwhile innovation, but so far there is nothing in the experience of the Department of Defense with incentive contracts to justify much optimism. Just as the HMOs require governmental funding, so incentive reimbursement contracts for hospitals depend on how the bureaucracy determines the class into which a hospital is placed and the other rules and regulations which it adopts. Certainly, the market is not the operative mechanism.

The foregoing illustrations point up the limitations encountered in seeking greater efficiency through new patterns of physician care or hospital reimbursement either by social intervention (HMOs) or market mechanisms (incentives). New approaches were next tried in financing the education of health professionals. No sooner had Congress passed legislation in 1971 to provide broad federal support for the education of health professionals[25] than the Administration became aware that the supply of these groups was turning around and that the long-term shortage of health manpower might shortly turn into a surplus. Accordingly, it began to explore how the federal government might extricate itself from a substantial financial commitment that might soon become dysfunctional.

The Administration's argument was simple: there were many more qualified applicants than places in schools of medicine, dentistry, and veterinary medicine. To ease their financial plight, the schools need merely to raise their tuition substantially and thus force the student or his family to pay the true cost of his education. This would enable the federal government to withdraw its support. Such a shift in financing would have to be accompanied by the establishment of adequate loan funds and additional scholarships for the disadvantaged, and the Administration pledged to make these funds available concurrently with the removal of general institutional support. The logic behind this proposal was reinforced by the recognition that health professionals could look forward to higher earnings than any other professional group in the society. It is anomalous to ask the taxpayer to subsidize the training of individuals who, shortly after they complete their studies, will be able to earn two to three times more than those who paid for their education.

But Congress refused to adopt a plan that would give an even greater advantage to the sons and daughters of upper class parents and that would saddle those from modest-income homes with heavy debts at graduation.

Another area in which the federal government has sought to

introduce more competition is in its campaign to get physicians to prescribe generic drugs rather than rely on brand
names. The price differential between many generic and
brand-name drugs is often substantial, and federal administrators, looking for economies, have begun to press physicians to
prescribe, and institutions to purchase, drugs by their generic
names. But the opposition from the pharmaceutical industry
and from certain physicians has been substantial. The opponents contend that when considerations of quality, reliability,
and related factors are taken into account, brand-name and generic drugs are not true equivalents. The argument remains in
suspense, since there is no way to determine the dollar value of
the admitted but still elusive quality variable.

During the past years, the federal judiciary has also moved
along the same track and attempted to increase competition in
the health care industry by proscribing certain long-standing
arrangements among providers that in the name of protecting
the consumer have actually confronted him with a monopoly.
Specifically, the judiciary has supported the efforts of individual plaintiffs and governmental regulatory bodies, such as the
Federal Trade Commission, to permit advertising by health
professionals, to enable commercial laboratories to compete
with units operated by physicians, and to restrict the power of
health professional societies to prescribe actions that are
directed more to protecting their members than protecting the
public.

These federal efforts to broaden the role of competition in
the health care industry are to be assessed less in terms of outcomes than intentions. On no front—the delivery of health
care, the reimbursement of hospitals, the production of health
manpower, the purchase of drugs—has the federal government achieved a clear-cut victory. Far from it. Most of the efforts have been marginal, have been aborted, or must yet

prove themselves. But the fact remains that in recent years each of the three branches of the federal government has tried to force the health care industry to operate more competitively.

This is the first part of the story. But there is another side. At the same time that the federal government has sought to increase reliance on the market in an effort to contain costs, increase consumer choice, and restrict opportunities for monopolistic exploitation, it has also moved in the opposite direction and has increased the role of administrative officials in almost every arena. A few illustrations will illuminate the strong forces operating in favor of increased reliance on governmental planning and control mechanisms.

In the final negotiations over Medicare, Congressional and Administration leaders reassured the American Medical Association that the new legislation would not alter the basic pattern governing the delivery of health care to the American people. But within relatively few years, the federal government had established additional control and direction over the health care industry. It stipulated the fee schedule at which it would reimburse physicians for services rendered to its beneficiaries. It sought to constrain the rate of hospital expansion and new construction by stipulating that it would provide reimbursement for only those Medicare patients who were treated in new beds approved by the appropriate state hospital authority. As noted earlier, Congress insisted that physicians organize themselves on a local or state basis and establish a review process to assess their treatment of Medicare and Medicaid patients who were hospitalized. It began to tie its continued support for the training of health manpower more closely to reciprocal commitments to underserved populations by the schools and the students who had received support.

The federal government's actions with respect to health

manpower were perhaps the most challenging, if only because they have brought it ever closer to a collision with the academic community, which places a high value on its freedom from outside direction. In its 1971 health manpower legislation, Congress decided to intervene directly for the first time in graduate medical education by providing funds for residency training programs in family care.

On a related front, the government established the National Health Service Corps as a way of attracting practitioners to underserved areas. The government provides special incentives to enrollees in the National Health Service Corps, including the repayment of educational loans that they had contracted in medical school. Subsequently, an extensive scholarship program to attract medical students was added. And in its 1976 health manpower legislation, the government intervened even further by stipulating the goals that the medical schools and their teaching hospitals had to reach by 1980 with respect to the training of specialists and family care physicians, the mandatory admission for clinical training of Americans who satisfactorily complete their preclinical studies abroad, and other detailed matters that hitherto had not been the government's prerogative.

And there have been other major interventions by government, both federal and state, in recent years. Thus in the last few years, a growing number of states have begun to establish some system of control over hospital beds, services, and rates. Today, in most large states, a hospital cannot be established or expanded unless the trustees have obtained prior approval from the appropriate state authority. And in many jurisdictions, this also applies to the establishment of a new service, such as open heart surgery or cobalt therapy or the purchase of expensive new equipment such as the CAT scanner, which costs about $600,000 per unit and has an annual operating cost of over $200,000. Some jurisdictions, such as New York State, have set lower limits on occupancy rates for different hospital services—for example, obstetrics or pediatrics. If occupancy rates fall below the established limits, the hospitals will not be reimbursed for care rendered on that service on the ground that low occupancy contributes to high costs and poor quality.

The most radical interventions relate to moves that would enable the federal and state governments to back away from the long-established practice of reimbursing hospitals for their costs, a practice that many lawmakers believe is the single biggest contributor to health cost escalation. To date, the approach has been to set limits on reimbursement—sometimes tight ones, as during the price and wage controls of 1971–74, sometimes looser ones, such as the new capping proposals of the Carter Administration. Since the hallmark of a competitive market is the full play of forces of demand and supply to determine prices, these ambitious government efforts to intervene and set limits on price increases represent a striking deviation from the market philosophy.

The efforts by government to intervene go further. During recent years, the federal authorities have exercised close control over the drug industry because of periodic evidence that inadequate testing by manufacturers prior to introducing a product has sometimes resulted in serious illness, and occasionally even in death. Some critics believe that governmental surveillance has become excessive, since current regulations mandate that when experiments involving human subjects are undertaken, each product must carry multiple safeguards requiring repeated trials, which in turn means increased expenditures of time and money. While some market enthusiasts argue that the effort at closer supervision of the drug industry is ill-conceived and slows medical progress un-

duly, there are other less doctrinaire critics, who are also concerned that the increasingly tight controls may be dysfunctional. Not even the prohibition of all new drugs would protect the consumer, since he, or the physician acting on his behalf, would seek to obtain drugs in use in other countries that appear to be effective even if the final verdict is not in. Clearly, the nation must attempt to find the appropriate balance between a market environment that stimulates the pharmaceutical industry to continue its research and development efforts for new and better drugs, and the clear necessity for reasonable procedures that protect consumers against inadequately tested products and devices.

Occasionally, government has been forced to act by the failure of the market, as happened in several states when commercial insurance companies withdrew from writing malpractice policies. An interesting by-product of the rash of successful malpractice suits has been the cost escalation resulting from the way in which physicians practice. Many have found it the better part of wisdom to practice defensively; that is, to order X rays and tests that in a quieter day they would have considered unnecessary. But, faced with the prospect of having to defend themselves in court, they consider it the safer course to underpin their decision-making—even if it means an added 10 to 20 percent to the costs of providing care.

No more telling argument against the market approach to reform of the health care industry can be found than the National Health Planning and Resources Development Act (PL 93-641) passed by Congress in 1974. This legislation provided a framework for an integrated governmental structure, with nongovernmental groups participating, at each level from the federal government down to the health service area (HSA). Implicit in this planning act was the growing conviction of Congress that the industry could not meet the needs of the public if it were left to its own devices. Secondly, Congress saw a place for federal initiative to start the planning process or, more correctly, to help it along, since it had already been underway in many jurisdictions. Thirdly, Congress implicitly acknowledged that the effective reform of health care delivery could not be accomplished by government alone, even if all three levels of government were closely aligned. Reform would be effective only if there were continuing participation between the governmental and nongovernmental sector, including hospitals, physicians, and consumer representatives.

Thus the planning act faces both ways. It gives new and added responsibilities to the governmental apparatus to influence the future directions of health care delivery. At the same time, it recognizes the need for active participation by the principal nongovernmental interest groups, particularly physicians, hospitals, and consumers.

It would be easy to conclude that this fluidity in philosophy and policy is further evidence of the ignorance and greed of politicians more concerned with retaining power than with finding effective solutions. A more charitable and also more valid interpretation would be that neither market nor plan alone can bring about the important reforms that the American people seek, even if they are unsure about how to achieve them. The answers may come slowly, but they are more likely to be right if we understand more about how the system operates before seeking heroic solutions.

Part Two

Goals

5

Access

HEALTH CARE is essentially an interchange between a patient (or his or her family acting as surrogate for a child or incapacitated adult) in search of a service and a provider able and willing to furnish it. Except under compulsory circumstances, such as a medical inspection in the Armed Services, the decision to initiate the interchange must be the patient's. Unless he or she makes the first move, there will be no encounter regardless of how many providers are able and willing to furnish care.

Nevertheless, in the design and redesign of health care systems, little attention has been paid to the role and responsibility of the citizen-patient. Yet we know that certain individuals and groups are reluctant to seek medical care. Some of these are restrained by their religious beliefs. Others find physicians, and particularly hospitals, threatening and therefore consistently avoid them. Some people, again for neurotic reasons, tend to disregard obvious symptoms, such as unusual bleeding or a lump in the breast, hoping that the symptom will resolve itself without medical attention. Because of the difficulties and costs of studying health care attitudes and behaviors of a large and diverse population, we know little about the conditions under which individuals seek medical attention or the extent to which, for psychological reasons, they fail to seek diagnosis and treatment.

We know that Christian Scientists generally do not seek or accept the help and care of physicians. Yet they are able to buy life insurance at rates no different from those offered to other people of the same age and occupational category. Superficially, it appears that access to medical services is less important than many of us assume. In the above instance, other behavioral patterns, such as a heightened degree of self-discipline, a lower incidence of alcoholism and smoking, and the emotional support from faith itself, may often compensate for lack of medical treatment.

Most reformers have focused attention on the other elements in the health equation; that is, on people who recognize that they need medical attention but are unable to obtain it or can do so only with difficulty. The classic barriers that have been identified are the nonavailability of providers and the inability of potential patients to pay for the services that are available.

The issues involved in access to health care are not confined to the responsibility of the patient, his need for financial resources, and the availability of providers. Conservatives have argued that the complete removal of the money barrier between patient and physician would result in "overloading" the health care system. Many individuals would crowd physicians' offices, clinics, even hospitals, not in response to threatening physical conditions that require professional attention, but because of a fear of illness and the need for reassurance. This group, estimated to account for one-third or more of all patients who seek medical consultation, has been dubbed the "worried well."

It is easier to quote statistics that support a position than to reach a balanced judgment about what it comprises or how to interpret it. We have already noted that the conservatives who opposed the introduction of Medicare warned that the system would be swamped by elderly patients. But as we saw, their fears did not materialize.

On the other hand, in the Province of Quebec, once the payment barrier was lowered, the demand for ambulatory services from the low-income population increased by about 15 percent, the same order of increase as that following the introduction of Medicaid in our own country.[26]

It would be easy to pile up evidence to prove either side of this argument. In Quebec, appointments are more difficult to arrange, and the amount of time that the physician spends with each patient has been reduced. On the other hand, patients now obtain services from providers to whom they formerly did not have access. It is easier to support one's ideological preference than to unravel the interactions that occur in a dynamic society after a radical change has been made in the mechanism of payment for health care.

Medical experts do not agree that one can or should distinguish sharply between patients whose complaints are unequivocally organic and those driven by anxiety or other emotional ills to seek the advice of physicians. It can be argued that in a post-Freudian era it is anachronistic to deny medical attention to hypochondriacs; such people are not well and may benefit from treatment. Moreover, pathology cannot be neatly differentiated into somatic and emotional, since both are often present; authorities contend that no somatic illness is ever completely free of emotional overlay. Others argue differently. They hold that in a world of scarce resources it is not feasible for the medical profession to provide care, reassurance, or support for the large numbers who periodically or continuously need help. Even if there were enough providers to permit professional care for all of the "worried well," such a step might still not be advisable, since psychotherapy, at its present stage of development, is not able to bring relief to many of these patients and may, in fact, serve to perpetuate their symptoms so that they will continue to seek treatment. The most cogent objection, however, stresses the distortions that would result from the diversion of so much staff time and effort from patients who most need attention to those with minor functional problems.

The basis of this distinction between the sick and the "worried well" is an important issue. Who in a society is to determine whether and when a person is entitled to seek medical attention? In a democratic society, especially one based on consumer sovereignty such as ours, any individual able to pay his physician's fee (or entitled to treatment under a government program) is free to seek medical attention. True, he cannot admit himself to a hospital or insist upon a specific therapeutic regimen. Nonetheless, if he can afford the price of a visit or if the government will pay for it, he can gain access to the system. This freedom would be curtailed if the "worried well" were to be differentiated from the sick. Who in that case would do the sorting and how much reliance could be placed on it?

There are many subtle as well as overt manifestations of the issue of access to medical care. We know that providers can stimulate or discourage individuals from seeking—or prolonging—treatment. In admitting and discharging patients, hospitals will act differently when their beds are close to full occupancy than in the months of low utilization. The same contrast can be found in the behavior of physicians. One who has more patients than he can handle is more likely to tell his patient to ring him after a few days and let him know how he is doing, while those who are struggling to build up practices are more likely to recommend that the patient return for a follow-up visit.

Current debate in the United States over inadequate access centers upon two considerations—locational and financial factors that preclude some families from receiving the same attention and care as others.

The first complaint about inadequacy of access concerns rural communities. Both members of Congress and state legislators are under constant pressure from rural constituencies that fear they will have no doctor when their elderly general practitioner retires. Other communities have been without a physician for years, unsuccessful in their efforts to recruit one despite their offer to provide well-equipped facilities, supporting help, and an assured income.

Congressmen and state legislators who seek help for their rural constituents in their efforts to attract a physician for the community often buttress their claim for governmental intervention by stressing the malfunctioning of the market. They point out that in 1973, 134 counties had no resident physician in active practice, and that the combined population of these counties totaled .5 million.[27] But the critical issue of access has less to do with geographic boundaries than with the ease or difficulty (in terms of time and money) with which a patient can reach a physician or a hospital. Using that criterion, we find that no more than 2 percent of the nation's population lives beyond one hour's drive from a health provider.[28]

It makes a considerable difference for public policy whether most of the 50 million persons living in non-urban areas encounter serious difficulties in obtaining access to the health care system or whether the true figure is a few million.

Clearly, the needs of the latter cannot be disregarded, but the scale of the remedial effort required is less formidable.

Even then, before concluding that government has a clear-cut obligation to intervene on behalf of the isolated rural minority, we should consider a question that has been posed by Aaron Wildavsky.[29] Since many of these people live in remote areas by choice, he asks, is government unequivocally obligated to provide essential services? The federal government has long recognized its obligation to provide medical care to members of the Merchant Marine, the Armed Services, veterans with service-connected disabilities, prisoners, and Indians who live on reservations—groups to whom the federal government has had a historic commitment. But people who live in outlying areas have thus far had no comparable claim for special consideration. Should they? Extending the argument further, Wildavsky points out that in many instances rural populations might have greater need for a lawyer to protect their property than they have for a physician, yet no one has suggested that it is a federal or state responsibility to provide ready access to members of the bar.

The issue is more complex than governmental action to provide a physician for all outlying areas, difficult as this would be. After all, a single physician, even one supported by a nurse or a technician, can provide little more than primary care. In the event of a complicated diagnostic problem or an intricate therapeutic procedure, medical or surgical, the patient would need the services of a larger center with a greater concentration of health resources. A competent local practitioner can at best screen those who require referral from those he is able to treat himself.

This distinction between the therapy an isolated practitioner can provide and the capabilities of a general hospital serves to emphasize the difference between expanding the number of health practitioners and improving the organizational structure of the delivery system. Increasing the number of physicians, including those who settle in out-of-the-way rural communities, is but one solution to the access problem. Another equally important solution involves the patient referral process. This has long been a skeleton in the closet of health reform because most physicians are understandably reluctant to make referrals that may, and often do, result in their losing both patient and income. But if a physician, whatever his rationale, treats patients whose conditions are beyond his knowledge and technique, the local population is not necessarily better off for having access to him than if they had to travel to a medical center.

The intractability of the whole problem is illustrated by the experience of foreign governments that have attempted to meet this challenge. The Soviets have stressed the importance of developing a nationwide health system, yet their coverage of rural areas is far from optimal. And the Bulgarian government, despite the offer of attractive incentives such as superior living quarters, a high cash income, and the promise of subsequent specialty training, has been unsuccessful in luring young physicians into rural practice. In Yugoslavia many newly graduated physicians, rather than being posted to outlying areas, are determined to remain in the capital, working at any type of job they can find—if necessary, limiting their medical practice to work at night, weekends, and vacations, when they can moonlight—while they wait—sometimes for years—for a suitable professional assignment. In their view, anything is better than exile to the countryside.

Israel boasts of more physicians per capita—about 1:500—than any other country in the world. Its health care system is operated by the trade union movement (Histadrut), which treats physicians no differently from other employees.

Yet although few settlements are more than one hour's distance from a major city, Israel has been unable to persuade more than an occasional physician to locate in a rural area.

This universal aversion on the part of physicians to rural practice is based on the same complex of forces: the young physician's desire to work close to the center of the medical establishment—the urban hospital and the university—which alone provides opportunities for specialty training; his predilection for colleague support and interaction; his need for technical resources, from laboratories to specialized diagnostic equipment; the prospects of developing an affluent practice; his preference for rearing his children in a more sophisticated environment; and the resistance of his wife to a rural life. All these factors lead physicians to sink roots in urban places.

Indeed, this aversion of most physicians to practicing in a rural area explains the steady outflow of young medical school graduates from the less developed countries, first in search of training, later in search of permanent relocation. Although many reformers believe that the United States has actively recruited these young physicians, the truth is that most of them are desperately seeking appointments abroad because they cannot be absorbed at home, not even in rural areas if they were willing to establish a rural practice. Without drugs, with no trained paramedics, with people too poor to seek medical attention, what kind of a practice could the young clinician establish in a developing country? The brain drain has less to do with the avariciousness of affluent countries than with the poorly designed medical training characteristic of most developing countries.

But returning to the problems of access to health care encountered by the rural population within the United States, there is the further problem of cultural attitudes and finances. People's willingness to seek health care is influenced by devel-

opments in medicine, the economy, and the larger society—
that is, they are more likely to seek physicians (1) when physicians are able to respond effectively, (2) if they have more
disposable income (or more insurance) at their command,
and (3) when news of modern medical successes is widely disseminated. While all of these factors have characterized the
country at large over the past decades, the rural population still
lags behind the rest of the country with respect to each.

The rural areas contain the largest number of families with
low incomes, and more of these families live in states that have
been unable or unwilling to provide adequate health services.
To illustrate the last point: in July 1975 the maximum family
income for federal participation in Medicaid was set at $2,200
and $2,400 for a family of four in Tennessee and Arkansas respectively; at $4,900 and $5,600 in Utah and North Dakota;
and at $6,400 and $6,500 in New York and Connecticut.[30]
These figures hold the clue to the less favorable data about the
access to health care of the rural population, which on the
average continues to lag behind the rest of the population in
both ambulatory visits and hospital admissions. However, the
gap between the rural and urban population has narrowed
since the institution of Medicaid, despite the much lower income ceilings characteristic of most of the Southern states.

But although access to health care in many rural areas remains a problem for which no ready solution is at hand, the
crux of the access issue lies in the inner cities, which house
large numbers of low income families, many of whom have
only recently settled there and have not yet adjusted, others
who do not speak English, and some of whom may be in the
country illegally. Paradoxically, the inner city is also the location of the nation's foremost teaching hospitals, with their sizable staffs of physicians and allied health manpower. But the
inner city lacks private practitioners, most of whom have relo-

cated to the suburbs to be closer to their more affluent patients or who have retired from active practice.

The small number of private practitioners located in low-income areas implies that ghetto residents will find it difficult and often impossible to be treated by a physician of their own choosing; one, for instance, with whom they can communicate easily. Another measure of inadequate access is the long waiting times associated with treatment in emergency rooms and outpatient clinics of nearby hospitals that they increasingly rely on for care.

The scheduling of clinic hours is a further deterrent, especially for individuals who are regularly employed. Since most clinics are not open in the evening or on weekends, a working man or woman must frequently forego a half and sometimes a full day's pay when seeking treatment.

Still another impediment for many low-income mothers is the problem of arranging for the care of children at home while they seek treatment for themselves or another family member at a clinic. For the handicapped or the aged there are the hazards of public transportation. And many patients who are not English-speaking often have difficulty in making themselves understood (while others who are English-speaking often encounter difficulties when assigned to a foreign medical graduate who is just learning the language).

These access problems arise less from locational inequalities than from a complex of socio-economic factors. Clearly, geographic propinquity between patients and providers is no guarantee of ready access. Even if distance were no barrier, formidable obstacles would often persist.

For many years critics of the health care system have stressed that inadequate income deprives a considerable part of the population of adequate access to care. This was certainly the case before Medicare and Medicaid. In 1964, the year before the passage of Medicare and Medicaid, about 28 percent of the poor had not seen a physician during the past two years compared to only 18 percent of the nonpoor. Among the nonwhite poor, the percentage reached 33. The nonpoor average was 4.6 visits to physicians a year, only slightly less for the poor (4.3) and considerably less for the nonwhite poor (3.1). The greatest discrepancy was found in dental visits per person per year: the nonpoor's total came to 1.8, more than double the 0.8 for the poor. Only in hospital discharges per 100 persons per year was the utilization rate higher for the poor than for the nonpoor: 13.8 versus 12.6 (although the nonwhite poor had a rate of only 9.9).[21] In inspecting these figures, it is important to allow for the fact that a higher than average proportion of persons with medical conditions requiring attention is likely to be found among the poor. Hence, other things being equal, the utilization rate of the poor should have been higher.

By 1973, eight years after the passage of Medicare and Medicaid, utilization of medical services among the entire population had increased and the gap in the rate of utilization among poor and nonpoor and among whites and nonwhites had been narrowed. A few summary findings: the proportion of the population that had not seen a doctor in the preceding two years had dropped for the nonpoor but much more rapidly for the poor, including the nonwhite poor. On the basis of short-stay hospital discharges, the poor showed half again as high a utilization rate in 1973 as the nonpoor, with the nonwhite poor making considerably more use of hospitals than nonpoor whites. In terms of doctor visits per person, the poor, including the nonwhites, moved ahead to 5.6 visits annually compared to 4.9 for the nonpoor. With respect to dental visits, the closing of the gap proceeded more slowly, but the poor showed a gain of about 35 percent and there was no increase in the average number of visits for the nonpoor.[21]

The conclusion that emerges as unequivocal is that Medicare and Medicaid made it easier for the poor to secure health services; by 1973, most of the indices show that the poor used more care than the nonpoor. One must be careful not to conclude from this that the poor are in a preferred position with respect to access. Unless their health needs relative to those of the nonpoor are known, no such conclusion is warranted. But we can safely conclude that the gap between them and the nonpoor has narrowed.

Still, before we can make a sweeping conclusion that financial barriers to health care have been removed, several caveats are in order. A poor family, hard-pressed to cover essentials such as food, rent, transportation, and other work-related costs, is likely to continue to cut corners when illness strikes. In the absence of a medical emergency, the poor will resort to home remedies, limit physician contacts, and skimp on follow-up care.

Moreover, we need to distinguish between the poor and the near-poor. We noted earlier the marked differences among the states in eligibility requirements for Medicaid. But, at whatever level they are set, families just above the cut-off point are likely to encounter substantial difficulties in covering their medical expenses, difficulties that have increased over the years because of the insistence of providers—clinics, hospitals, and physicians—on payment for all services. Prior to the passage of Medicaid, each of these providers had traditionally offered a large amount of free or below cost services, which meant that many patients were able to get care for whatever they could afford to pay. But now that government covers such a high percentage of the costs of welfare patients, providers have become accustomed to seeking full, or close to full, payment for all.

Access for the poor, although it has been eased by Medicaid, is also shaped by the availability of provider institutions.

To illustrate: for the ghetto population of Chicago, the principal medical resource is Cook County Hospital with its large inpatient and clinic facilities. In New York the inner city population has recourse to a sizable municipal hospital system and also is able to use the resources of the large number of nonprofit teaching hospitals, which because of their large endowments have been able to provide many free or below cost services to the medically indigent. These teaching hospitals have increasingly become community hospitals so that in 1975 they accounted for just under half of all discharged hospital patients.

Other aspects of the issue of access are worth noting. Among younger age groups, the proportion of pregnant women who fail to receive adequate prenatal and postnatal care and the proportion of children who do not receive basic preventive services are surprisingly high. Most of these problems are found among the lowest income groups, particularly among minorities. Given the availability of Medicaid, however, this inadequate utilization of prenatal, postnatal, and preventive health services by the poor appears to stem from the inadequate linkage between these groups and health care institutions rather than from a deficiency in income or entitlement to care.

Despite Medicare, there are special problems that senior citizens face in obtaining health services. Many older persons who are partially or totally immobile cannot find a physician who is willing to care for them in their homes. Others who are in nursing homes often lack adequate medical or nursing care. And those who are not certified for Medicaid often encounter difficulties in meeting their share of medical costs under Medicare.

Clearly, this discussion has not exhausted those instances where financial barriers continue to block ready access to

health care. It is certainly true that over a wide range of income levels a sizable number of individuals and families obtain
less care than they need because of insufficient means and
because government has not assumed responsibility to provide
it for them. But, as we have seen, there is another side to the
issue of access. Now that the financial barriers to obtaining
care have been substantially lowered, other factors such as education, life style, and socialization account for much of the
continuing difficulty for low-income families.

A final yet fundamental caveat. Implicit in most discussions
of health system reform is the assumption that "more is better"; consequently, greater access is equated with an increased
volume of medical services for the individual. We know, however, that most visits to physicians are made for self-limiting
conditions from which a patient will usually recover following
a brief period of bed rest or limitation of activity. In a few instances, the intervention provided by the physician, such as
the prescription of antibiotics, not only fails to help but may
actually retard recovery because of unforeseen side effects.
The same is true for more definitive inpatient treatment.
Whereas many procedures may be essential, in other instances
the balance between risk and benefit is not clearly perceived by
the physician, much less by the patient. Though definitive
data are lacking, it is estimated that thousands of patients die
every year and many more suffer serious disabilities because of
medical or surgical interventions for conditions that they
would have been willing to tolerate had they been informed of
the risk involved. A major task that faced the Surgeon General
of the Army during World War II was to proscribe a range of
aggressive therapies whose pursuit was contraindicated by
the excessive risk-benefit ratio associated with them.

Finally, the issue of access forces a reconsideration of the
limits of the health care system. In the last several decades,
hundreds of thousands of persons suffering from alcoholism

have joined Alcoholics Anonymous, and in the process many of them have been cured. Yet their involvement is not reflected in any of the conventional data on access. Similarly, a substantial number of persons have in recent years been involved in programs designed to cure them of drug addiction. Many have been freed of their addiction; others have been helped to switch to a less dangerous drug. For the most part, these encounters are not included in reports on health services.

Another parallel development relates to the large numbers of persons who have joined or are currently enrolled in programs aimed at improving their mental health and emotional well-being. It is easy to ridicule many of these programs as lacking in theory and therapy—or even to charge that they are a mild disguise for sexual experiences among strangers. But others cannot be so easily dismissed. A cautious assessment would have to acknowledge that they make some contribution to the emotional well-being of at least some of the participants.

These extensions greatly add to the complexity of the access issue, especially if they include the educational advice offered by science writers to the consumer about his health and health habits, from urging men to exercise to encouraging women to be periodically examined for cancer of the breast or cervix.

These last considerations suggest that what sometimes appears to be a simple question of access to health services turns out to be closely related to people's understanding about caring for their health, which includes seeking medical attention when they need it. In the past decade, the United States has taken major steps to lower the financial barriers to health care. Although some financial barriers remain, they are probably less important than a host of attitudinal and behavioral characteristics that largely determine what people are able and willing to do to protect their health and to seek professional help when they need it.

6

Quality

TURNING from the issue of access to the issue of quality is a logical and necessary step, since there would be little justification for broadening access if it entailed a substantial reduction in the quality of the services that physicians offer their patients. All propositions about the output of the health care system must consider quality as an essential dimension of service. Professionals know that in the absence of an acceptable standard of quality, medical intervention may not only fail to help the patient but may actually harm him. The public, aware that it cannot judge professional competence, has pressed for various assessment mechanisms to assure that the quality of care is satisfactory.

What then are some of the complex and unresolved issues with respect to quality that are engaging or should engage the public as it attempts to reform the health care industry?

The beginning of wisdom is to recognize that the evaluation of quality is inherently subjective. This helps to explain why one patient will praise a physician whom another has found wanting. And each may be right. Since the efficacy of any medical intervention almost always involves reassurance and support, which in turn depend on the interaction between patient and physician, what in one instance can turn out to be good rapport may in another case lead to distrust or heightened anxiety.

There are other subjective elements in the assessment of health services. What one provider recommends, another may disapprove. Since there is frequently no way to make an objective assessment of the effectiveness of a particular intervention, each physician must draw on his own training and experience, and these often differ. This fact explains, at least partially, why physicians are loath to criticize one another.

Another difficulty in assessing quality stems from the dynamic nature of medical progress. Accepted practices in one period—say, the almost universal practice of removing tonsils in young children a generation ago—are no longer accepted. If the time period is lengthened and we consider medical practices of the last century rather than the last generation, we know today that physicians who bled their patients prolonged their illnesses and frequently speeded their deaths. Awareness that current therapies are constrained by the existing state of knowledge—some part of which will certainly be proved wrong at some time in the future—helps to explain why some consumers seek out physicians who practice conservatively.

Significant differences in medical practices also exist among countries at the same general level of development as well as in different regions of the same country. While certain standards of quality, such as asepsis, transcend national and regional boundaries, others are essentially culture-bound. Several years ago I learned that some members of the U.S. Embassy staff in Stockholm sought routine health care abroad because they objected to the brusque attitudes and manner of

Swedish practitioners. They were accustomed to more considerate treatment, although, as one informant noted, "apparently the Swedes didn't mind."

A more complex aspect of the quality issue derives from the way in which health care systems are structured. Compare, for example, the situation in the United States and the United Kingdom. In the United States it is customary for the primary physician to retain responsibility for the care of a patient who has been hospitalized. In the United Kingdom community-based (general) care and hospital-based (specialty) care are separated, and the primary physician withdraws from the case when a specialist admits the patient to the hospital.

The U.S. system has the distinct advantage of permitting the patient's regular physician, if he is fortunate enough to have one, to participate in every phase of the decision-making, from initial diagnosis to rehabilitation. Often the family physician is able to contribute to the treatment plan even when the patient is under the direct care of a specialist. On the other hand, the sharp differentiation in the United Kingdom between general practitioners on the outside and consultants (specialists) who are hospital-based also has some strong points. Thus there is greater assurance that those who are responsible for surgery or other complex forms of treatment are fully qualified. In the United States one of the recognized problems in assuring the quality of medical care is the considerable number of physicians who undertake procedures beyond their qualifications and experience.

In recent years much attention has been drawn to the fact that the ratio of neurosurgeons to population is about seven times greater in the United States than in the United Kingdom.[31] From this and other statistics, it has been inferred that an excessive volume of neurosurgery is performed in the United States. But the matter is more complicated than such gross differences in manpower ratios would suggest. First, one would have to take account of how the work load is divided among different types of specialists (such as neurosurgeons, orthopedic surgeons, and neurologists) in the two countries; and second, one would have to consider the differences between the two countries in accepted indications for neurosurgery. For instance, in the United States surgery for the relief of certain types of intractable pain is approved practice; it is less common in the United Kingdom.

Within the United States there are also important differences among regions. For example, Medicare patients in the South are half as likely to undergo surgery as those in the Northeast.[32] But it is not easy to reach a judgment concerning the quality of care solely on the basis of this striking difference, since the decision to operate on an older person involves both professional judgment and patient preference. Cultural attitudes in the two regions may be sufficiently different not only to explain but to justify these variations in medical practice.

Such differences between countries and among regions of the same country concerning accepted types of medical interventions do not mean that these are insurmountable barriers to assessing the quality and raising the level of health care. They do, however, define a zone of uncertainty about the boundaries of professional practice within an evolving system of care.

Conventional efforts to improve the quality of health involve the education of health practitioners, the specification of standards governing the construction and use of facilities (including improved linkages among the components of the health care system), and various societal interventions designed to provide better assurance of quality.

The striking gains in the quality of American medicine during this century have been made primarily through improvements in the quality of medical education, first at the undergraduate level and more recently through graduate medical education. Between 1910 and 1930 it was possible, through the combined efforts of the American Medical Association and state legislatures, to eliminate all of what were then known as grade B schools. Indeed, in the entire history of this country it is hard to find a more influential social tract than the Flexner Report on American medical education. Released in 1910, this report carefully documented the sorry state of many schools and pointed out the directions for remedial actions.[33] These reforms resulted in all future physicians receiving a sound grounding in the biological underpinnings of medicine, in carefully graded educational experiences, and in well supervised internships. But no sooner had these gains been achieved than the advances in biomedical science and medical technology led to a further elevation of standards. The basic four-year undergraduate curriculum was extended to an approximately equal period of residency training as a prerequisite for a physician gaining certification as a specialist.

The high prestige and earnings of physicians have enabled the medical schools to pick from among the more able members of the college population. This, together with the schools' high ratio of teaching faculty to students, has contributed further to the establishment and maintenance of a high level of professional education.

When a physician joins a hospital staff, especially one that is selective in its appointments, he can continue his education through a range of experiences, from participating in clinical-pathological conferences, participating in rounds, and supervising and instructing residents, to taking advantage of the many other learning opportunities, formal and informal, that characterize the environment of a teaching hospital.

However, this stimulating and supportive environment for continuing professional growth is not available to all physicians. Some do not have a hospital appointment; others have privileges at small hospitals that do not have training programs; still others are attracted to staffs where there is little peer review of work. In short, one of the major factors contributing to indifferent and poor quality of health services reflects weaknesses in the working environment of many practicing physicians who do not have the opportunity or the desire to keep up-to-date.

Since a sizable, but unknown, proportion of American physicians practice under such conditions, there is ground for concern about the substantial influx of foreign medical graduates (FMGs) who have come here in ever larger numbers in recent years for residency training. The vast majority of these foreign graduates succeed in converting their visas to the status of permanent immigrants. The result is that, in a few states along the Eastern seaboard, they now comprise the majority of all newly licensed physicians. [34]

Leaders of the health professions, with an occasional assist from an interested legislator or newspaper reporter, have called attention to the anomaly of continuously strengthening American medical education while simultaneously permitting increasing numbers of less qualified graduates of foreign institutions to enter the profession through admission to U.S. residency training programs. Concern about these foreign medical graduates is grounded not only in their inferior undergraduate training, reflected in their poor performance on the examinations used to test the competence of American medical school graduates, but also in their lack of language skills, which makes it difficult for many of them to relate effectively to their patients. Most informed persons, for reasons previously noted, believe that foreign trained physicians provide, on the average, a lower quality of care.

The impact of foreign medical graduates on the quality of

care should be neither minimized nor exaggerated. It should not be minimized for they currently account for a large part of all newly licensed physicians. On the other hand, recent legislation (1976) requires that in the future foreign graduates pass the same examinations as graduates of American medical schools.

The changing realities of the FMG issue can be summarized as follows. The Department of State has issued a one-year blanket waiver in order to enable those FMGs with exchange-student visas to continue entering the United States under the 1976 Health Manpower Act. This source represents about 40 percent of the flow. The remaining 60 percent, who apply for admission as immigrants, no longer receive preferential treatment because medicine has been removed from the "critical shortage list." This regulation, together with the larger flow of American graduates into residency training, suggests that the problem has probably peaked.

Yet two critical questions, closely linked to the issue of quality, remain. To the extent that foreign-trained physicians have shown themselves more willing than U.S. trained physicians to practice in the least attractive institutions (state mental hospitals, prisons, ghetto clinics) and in the least attractive areas (low-income concentrations along the East Coast and in a few large urban centers in the Midwest), what will be the intermediate and long-term consequences of a significant reduction in their future numbers? Clearly, there is a need for careful monitoring to ensure that populations now served by these foreign physicians are not deprived of access to medical care. It is also important to ensure that the new federal regulations do not lead to the creation of an enlarged "medical underground" of unlicensed practitioners where quality controls will prove even more difficult to enforce.

There is a dearth of reliable data on the participation of

FMGs in residency training and almost no information about those who have completed or terminated such training and are currently in practice. It is noteworthy that both the American Medical Association and the American Hospital Association have consistently opposed legislation restricting FMGs and, when such legislation was imminent, proposed a gradual phase-in rather than an abrupt reversal of previous policy.

Establishing quality assurance through control of the educational preparation of health providers is a particular problem in the mental health care area. Here, the most intensively trained medical psychoanalyst, whose preparation often involves a decade or more of postgraduate education and personal and didactic analysis, competes with clinical psychologists, social workers, and even self-educated psychotherapists, who are permitted to counsel, advise, support, and otherwise serve the public. True, nonmedical counselors are constrained by law from engaging in certain types of intervention, from drug therapy to electric shock treatments. Moreover, there is a never-ending effort among the more professionally oriented of these groups to establish qualifications and standards, and several groups, including clinical psychologists and psychiatric social workers, have succeeded in becoming licensed in some states. The fact remains, however, that for each group that is licensed another, without recognized qualifications, emerges to compete at the fringes of the field.

The explanation for this state of affairs must be sought in the nonspecificity of many psychotherapeutic interventions. The law cannot interfere with a client's freedom to seek help from a counselor by talking through his problems. And it is difficult for government to specify legal qualifications for all who counsel. Statutory and administrative controls over the quality of health services, at least in the realm of mental health, cannot disregard the public's determination to seek and use assistance of its own choosing. As long as the psychotherapist does not engage in procedures that only licensed personnel are authorized to perform, he enjoys considerable freedom to pursue his practice in a way that is mutually satisfactory to his clients and himself.

The issue of quality takes on a different complexion in the case of surgery. Not only do the state, the medical profession, and the hospital exercise controls to ensure that only licensed physicians operate, but the specialty societies, with the assistance of hospital trustees, have long sought to restrict complicated procedures to those who have additional qualifications. Recently, the surgical leadership has proposed to restrict *all* hospital surgery to physicians who have been certified by the American Board of Surgery. Such a proposal, if accepted, will, it is argued, discourage unnecessary surgery, reduce the costs of health care and, most importantly, contribute to the quality of care by assuring that patients will be operated on only by fully qualified surgeons. Each of these claims has considerable merit. At the same time, it is difficult to ignore the fact that the proposal is advanced at a time when there is a growing awareness of the surplus of surgeons.

In recent years, it has been argued that significant gains in quality can be achieved only if the medical school curriculum is shifted from its preoccupation with biomedical knowledge to the psychological, humanistic, and sociological disciplines. Physicians, so runs the argument, should learn to treat the individual and his family in their home surroundings rather than solely as disease entities. They should learn to listen more, hear better, and be more responsive to what their patients say. To date, however, these recommendations have made little headway, and not because their merit is denied. But is it possible to teach the medical student these skills? And what would be the cost of such training if the student finished his medical studies poorly prepared to diagnose or treat organic disease?

There have been other changes in medical education, although their impact on the quality of health care is not clear. During the last decade, for example, there has been a large increase in the proportion of women and minority group members among the medical student body; the proportion of these two groups grew from under 10 percent to about 30 percent. We do not question the desirability of eliminating discrimination based on sex or race in the selection of applicants for medical school. However, we must question the claim that altering the composition of the profession by including more women and blacks will inevitably raise the quality of care. Women and blacks may bring to their practices special sensitivities related to their sex or race. But considerable time must pass before their career patterns—in terms of the graduate training they pursue, their choice of a location at which to practice, etc.—are revealed. Until then, clear-cut gains in quality remain putative rather than proved.

One of the most troublesome issues directly affecting quality assurance is that small number of practitioners who, no matter how well they have been trained, develop personality disorders or other aberrant behavior that jeopardize their patients' health and welfare. These pathologies range from drug or alcohol addiction to physicians undertaking procedures beyond their competence or submitting patients to unnecessary procedures for pecuniary gain. Although it is inevitable that any professional group with some 400,000 members will contain a small proportion against whom disciplinary action would be justified, there is a strong tradition in medicine that keeps the profession from undertaking such action except in cases of the most egregious misconduct. Furthermore, in the absence of strong professional leadership, there is little scope for effective governmental action. In the Province of Quebec, physicians who earn more than$10,000 per month are called before their peers to explain the nature of a practice that results in such high earnings. In selected U.S. cities, local medical societies have made it easier for patients to register complaints about the improper behavior of their physicians, and a serious effort is made to investigate these charges and to take corrective action if they are substantiated. But such measures are the exception rather than the rule.

Up to this point we have been concerned with the education, training, and behavior of the physician only. By law, only the physician is authorized to treat patients; that is, to make the critical decisions on his patients' health and well-being. But the relationship between medical manpower and quality is not limited to the physician. One of the conspicuous trends in modern medicine has been the continuing diversification and specialization of health manpower to a point where there are now at least fifty distinct occupational categories. In 1974 approximately half of the 4.7 million persons active in the health professions were classified in "nursing and related services." Within that large group less than 860,000 were registered nurses; the largest number—936,000—were nursing aides, orderlies, or attendants; and about half a million were practical nurses.[8] As anyone who has recently been hospitalized will affirm, during the course of a single day it is likely that between ten and twenty persons other than members of the medical staff will do something for or to him—from drawing blood, taking his temperature, giving him medication, and "prepping" him for surgery to bringing or removing his food trays. Poor-quality care is not necessarily restricted to gross errors in medical intervention. It may reflect error by anyone in the extended hierarchy of the hospital staff. Although the number of hospital patients who receive the wrong medication or the wrong dosage is said to be substantial, the errors are fortunately only occasionally fatal.

Efforts to improve the competence of paraprofessional groups have been directed to two ends: raising the educational and training requirements for these groups and putting into place a tight system of supervision to oversee their work. But each of these approaches has its costs.

There are compelling reasons to train people only up to the level at which they will work or up to the level to which they may be advanced in the future. To do more is both costly to the employer and frustrating to the worker. In the health field, we may already have reached and even exceeded the optimal point in the division of labor. In the future, improvements in quality as well as reductions in personnel expenditures may well be achieved by hiring more highly qualified persons in order to cut the costs of supervision and gain greater flexibility in work assignments. This is the opinion of some experienced hospital administrators who believe that whenever the proportion of registered nurses drops to below 40 percent of their total nursing personnel, the efficiency of their services, including the critically important quality of nursing care, declines.

After personnel, the second dimension of quality assurance relates to facilities and how they are constructed, used, and coordinated. Not many years ago, large teaching hospitals, especially those in old buildings, had wards containing twenty or even thirty patients. With the introduction of Medicare, hospitals were encouraged to remodel their old wards and prohibited from building new ones by governmental reimbursement regulations that specified a maximum of four patients per room as the definition of semiprivate care.

In addition to straightforward regulations requiring hospitals to reduce and eliminate as far as possible fire and accident hazards, various health authorities, both governmental and voluntary, have long specified minimum acceptable conditions to assure improved quality, particularly in those areas of the hospital where the risks of infection are most likely to occur. These efforts at setting standards have unquestionably helped to raise the quality of the physical environment, but they have had only a minor influence on the quality of hospital care, which depends less on facilities and more on the treatment regimen.

Thus the Army's forward hospitals in World War II, Korea, and Vietnam practiced excellent medicine despite the temporary nature of most facilities. The essence of quality care consisted of getting the patient to the proper specialist as quickly as possible. The cornerstone of the Army medical system has been effective triage (distribution) and a high order of staff specialization. But tight control over the flow of patients cannot be easily achieved in civilian life, in which people are free to choose their own physicians, physicians and hospitals have an economic interest in where patients are treated, and the patient must weigh the gains and losses of visiting a local practitioner against seeking treatment in a distant community.

Although we know that the pull of the market draws patients from afar into the nation's principal medical centers, it is hard to identify other successful efforts at regionalization by which hospitals and health practitioners within an area are coordinated so that patients requiring specialized treatment can be concentrated in specialized institutions. Pittsburgh and Rochester, New York, have made such efforts, but they have had only modest success. A more typical picture is one of hospitals within the same community under different systems of control—private for profit, voluntary nonprofit, and governmental—that frequently offer disparate levels of care.

The inferior quality of most county or municipal hospitals compared to the average community nonprofit institution can be attributed to a variety of factors. Public hospitals usually operate on a lower per diem budget; nevertheless, they must accept all indigent patients who need care. Usually, they lack the support of committed trustees. Their administrators are hobbled by onerous civil service rules and regulations. Facilities and equipment are frequently poorly maintained. They have less attraction for professional staff and for other relatively scarce personnel such as registered nurses. All of these factors are not necessarily present, and they generally are not if the public hospital is linked to a medical school. In combination, however, they profoundly depress the level of care that such institutions are able to provide.

The quality of care available to the members of a community depends not only on the strength of the individual health care institution but on whether and to what extent patients are treated where they are most likely to benefit from care. A wide range of factors integral to both patients and hospitals— including social class, ability to pay, race, religion, the presence of a teaching program, the utilization rate, etc.—have operated to encourage, but often also to discourage, an optimal pattern of admissions.

But other differences in staffing, tradition, and cost remain. It is generally recognized that a small community hospital may have a competent staff, do little or no teaching, and charge only half as much as a major hospital center. As long as a patient has a simple condition such as the removal of an infected appendix or hemorrhoids and does not develop complications during his hospitalization, he may receive much the same quality of care in either institution. But if complications occur, the quality differential between the two institutions could prove critical.

A more complicated situation is reflected by efforts in recent years to improve the quality of emergency care available to the victim of a serious accident, heart attack, poisoning, or other life-threatening situation. Various levels of government, occasionally with foundation support, have experimented with improved ambulance service, sophisticated communications systems, the training of personnel, and above all with the identification of hospitals that can treat patients who need specialized care (major trauma cases). The follow-up studies suggest that because of the many interdependent variables involving staff, travel time, and specialization, clear-cut gains in quality resulting from the "rationalization" of emergency care still remain to be proved.[35]

In evaluating measures to improve quality, the evidence from foreign systems has been substantially ignored. It is rare for the health care literature to call attention to some of the more subtle aspects of quality, such as the prolongation of waiting time for appointments by middle-class patients that followed the institution of Medicare in the Province of Quebec during the early seventies. And only inadvertently does one learn how difficult it is for persons who become ill on a weekend in Sweden to obtain proper treatment. Then there is clogging of the hospitals of the National Health Service in Great Britain with chronically ill older patients who have no further need for specialized hospital care but for whom alternative facilities are unavailable; this results in a delay of up to a year or more for many elective procedures, including the repair of hernias. Nor is much written about the disgruntled trade union-employed clinic physician in Israel who often reports late for work and leaves early, causing many workers to be off the job for five hours while they wait to have an injured finger bandaged.

Such illustrations are not intended to denigrate the quality of health care in countries that have won the admiration of many U.S. observers. Rather, they are presented in the hope that in all discussions about restructuring the health care delivery system in this country, especially with regard to prepaid plans, the issue of quality control will be faced. Kaiser-Permanente has sought to respond to this challenge by requiring that its subscribers have a choice of care, such as Blue Cross and Blue Shield, available to them; in some locations, however, effective alternatives simply do not exist. The need for well-defined standards of quality in the implementation and operation of prepaid systems of care has been acknowledged by its chief designer, Dr. Paul Ellwood; yet these standards have not been formulated. In the absence of such standards, Congress, the public, and the enrollees will find it difficult to determine whether putative gains in efficiency are true improvements or merely reflect compromises in the quality of service provided.

The difficulties of ensuring quality in hospital care has led to new forms of societal intervention, most importantly the actions undertaken by third-party reimbursers and the establishment of Professional Standards Review Organizations (PSROs). By far, the most radical intervention affecting the entire health care system is the recently expanded federal manpower effort (1976) to shift the balance between specialists and primary care physicians in the direction of the latter.

Although the primary interest of third-party payors is cost control rather than quality control, the two are not independent. A specialized service that operates far below its optimum patient load is likely not only to generate unduly high costs but to provide care of inferior quality because of the limited experience of the staff. Hence third-party payors are increasingly linking hospital reimbursement to the maintenance of a minimum level of activity in such specialized services as obstetrics, intensive coronary care, and open heart surgery.

It is too early to reach even a preliminary judgment about

the ambitious Professional Standards Review Organization program enacted under the 1972 amendments to the Social Security Act. A few developments, however, can be anticipated. First, the availability of government funds will undoubtedly increase the number of hospitals that will systematically pursue utilization studies. Consequently, new systems will be introduced to reduce procedures and practices that are of uncertain value to the patient and that tend to increase costs.

What remains debatable is the extent to which the development and utilization of norms and criteria governing treatment may, by leading to excessive standardization, have unfortunate side effects. Conformity to established norms may discourage the exercise of independent professional judgment and stifle innovation. Moreover, since patients often have idiosyncratic reactions even to conventional therapies, uniformity could prove counterproductive. On the other hand, if allowance is made for such deviations, the introduction of norms may have no more than a marginal effect on practice or costs.

The most radical approach to quality assurance seeks to shift the distribution of physician manpower from specialists to generalists. Many in American medicine, in Congress, and among consumer groups believe that the quality of health care could be substantially improved if there were fewer specialists and more primary care physicians. Specialists keep fixed hours, they agree, and are less likely to respond when patients confront an emergency. In addition, they may recommend more complex procedures than the patient's condition warrants, since they desire to put their specialized techniques to use. Moreover, their specialization may lead them to overlook conditions that lie outside their area of special competence. Such arguments may have considerable validity without necessarily proving that the contemplated shift to more primary care physicians would be a clear-cut gain if it could be achieved. The fact is that we know too little about how specialists spend their time to reach a definitive conclusion about whether a changed distribution of physician manpower would result in improved care.

One final word: We cannot ignore, even though we cannot explore in depth, the relation between the quality of care and the overall goals of the health care system. Traditionally, these goals have been to prevent illness where it can be prevented and to restore the sick and injured so that they can again function effectively. Where medicine is unable to provide a cure, it has the obligation to lessen suffering and pain and to support the afflicted patient. More and more of contemporary medicine's efforts are being directed to the aged, those who not only cannot be returned to effective functioning but who live in the shadow of death. Among both the leaders of the profession and thoughtful citizens there is growing uncertainty about the meaning of quality under these changed circumstances.

A host of new issues has come to the fore. There is first the right of a patient suffering from an incurable disease to determine whether he may die without further efforts to prolong his life. The State of California has legislated the living will, which aims to protect the physician if the patient opts for the cessation of treatment. In Great Britain the professional advisers to the National Health Service have agreed on a range of radical interventions that will not be used for older patients on the ground that they are of dubious value and are too costly to the nation. The British have also established specialized facilities—hospices—in which terminally ill patients can spend their last weeks in cheerful surroundings where they receive good nursing care and emotional support to ease their anxieties about death. The facilities can be operated at a fraction of the cost of general hospital care.

These last sentences underscore the close links that exist,

even though they are not always recognized, between the health goals that a nation pursues, the quality standards it strives to achieve, and the total costs of health care that it is able and willing to underwrite. Discussions of quality are always linked to issues of cost. And it is to costs that we now turn.

7

Costs

THE PUBLIC has been made abundantly aware of the precipitous rise in the costs of health care since World War II; its concern now is that the trend persists unabated. In 1950 the nation spent just $12 billion, or 4.6 percent of the gross national product, for personal health care services. In Fiscal Year 1976 (from July 1975 through June 1976), according to an estimate of the Department of Health, Education and Welfare, the total bill came to $139 billion, or 8.6 percent of the GNP.[9]

Several developments between 1950 and 1976 help to explain and rationalize part—but only part—of this steep rise. In that period the nation's population grew from 151 million to 214 million, or over 41 percent. And the purchasing power of the dollar declined substantially, about 55 percent as measured by the consumer price index.[36] Correcting for these two factors, an expenditure in 1976 of approximately double the 1950 level—that is, about $24 billion—is indicated. That still leaves $115 billion to be accounted for.

Before examining these figures more closely, it may be use-

ful to identify some important structural changes of the past
quarter century that influenced the level of expenditures.

Let us start with physicians. In 1950 most physicians worked
long hours and provided considerable free services both to
private patients who were unable to pay their fees and to clinic
and ward patients in return for hospital privileges. In 1950
only a small minority of all private practitioners were board-
certified specialists. A quarter of a century later, these patterns
had changed. With the shift from general practice to specialization, the average physician raised his level of fees to reimburse him for his longer training and enhanced skills.

However, the fees that professionals command depend in
the final analysis on the ability and willingness of the consuming public to pay for their services. In this regard, several facts
are worth noting. The real per capita disposable income of the
American people, measured in constant 1972 dollars, increased from about $2,400 in 1950 to $4,000 in 1975, or by
approximately 70 percent.[36] As a result, Americans were able to
buy more health services without foregoing other essentials or
luxuries. Still, if we examine the changing consumption patterns of the population during this period, we find that although this enlarged real income was distributed over every
aspect of consumption, the *relative* expenditures for housing,
personal services, and health care increased.

And by far the steepest rise was in the area of health care. In
1950 per capita expenditure for physicians' services was less
than $18 a year; in 1975 this figure had risen to over $105, or
sixfold. In the beginning of the period, 85 percent of all spending for physicians' services was in the form of direct payments
from patients; by 1975 the share of direct payments had declined to just under 40 percent.[9] Two developments were
responsible for this shift. The first was the accelerated growth
of private insurance. By 1975, insurance companies ac-

counted for over 35 percent of all payments to physicians, a dramatic rise from 10 percent in 1950. There was a parallel increase in payments to physicians from public funds—from 5 percent to 25 percent during the period. Insurance and government, which together had accounted for only about one-sixth of all payments at the beginning of the period, were responsible for three-fifths at its end.[9]

Consumers must ration their expenditures, since they never have enough money to buy everything they need or desire. They constantly seek to optimize the benefits they can obtain with their limited dollars. The growth of health insurance introduced a new factor in the purchase of physicians' services. Many consumers no longer pay their physicians directly; since their outlays are covered by third-party payors, they are less likely to economize in the use of physicians' services. At the same time, the services that a patient obtains from his physician have not remained the same over the past three decades. Take the general check-up as an illustration. The physician uses more complex equipment, takes more tests, and involves more staff assistants—and all of this contributes to raising the cost of the examination. The rise in hospital costs has been even more precipitous.

In 1950, when payments for physicians' services amounted to $2.7 billion, or roughly 23 percent of total expenditures for health care, payments for hospital care were $3.7 billion, or 31 percent. By 1975, the hospital care component had risen to $48.2 billion, or 39 percent of the total.[9] Clearly, most of the health cost escalation during these years was linked directly to increased hospital costs.

A few additional facts and figures will provide perspective on these years. There was an insignificant increase in the number of hospitals, from under 6,800 to over 7,100, and a similarly insignificant increase in the total number of beds, from about

1.45 million to 1.53 million. These aggregate figures, however, obscure a substantial growth in the dynamic sector of the industry—the nonpublic short-term hospitals that provide most of the acute care people receive. These facilities increased from slightly over 5,000 to about 5,900, or by 18 percent; their bed complement grew even more substantially—from about 500,000 to 900,000, an increase of 80 percent. The ratio of such beds per 1,000 people increased from 3.3 to 4.3, or by a factor of one-third.[37]

This rise in short-term hospitals and beds laid the groundwork for a substantial rise in total expenditures. Once beds are built, the tendency is to fill them; even when they are not occupied, they contribute substantially to total costs. Experts have calculated that an empty bed incurs as much as 60 to 70 percent of the costs of an occupied bed.

After 1950 there was also a steady increase in the annual admission rate. In 1950, 110 admissions per 1,000 population were to a short-term hospital. By 1973, the figure stood at 160—up more than 45 percent. Admissions provide one clue to hospital use, but other criteria must also be taken into consideration. The total number of hospital days increased at a slower rate, from 1,165 days per 1,000 during these same years to 1,414, or by 21 percent. The moderating factor was the decline in the average length of stay from 10.6 days to 8.8, or by 17 percent. During the last quarter century, the hospital occupancy rate fluctuated only slightly, remaining in the middle to upper 70 percent range.[37]

Another factor that contributed to an increase in utilization and therefore in costs was the sizable expansion in the outpatient services of short-term hospitals. In the eight years between 1965 and 1973, the annual rate of outpatient visits rose from 640 to about 1,100 per 1,000 population.[37]

These are some of the trends that played a significant role in the public's greater reliance on hospital care in the decades following 1950. The significance of this increased utilization is clear. The average daily number of patients in short-term hospitals rose from 372,000 in 1950 to 681,000 in 1973, an increase of approximately 80 percent; and the number of patients admitted during the course of a year increased from 16.7 million to 31.8, or by some 90 percent.[37] Taking into account both the number of patients and days of care, short-term hospitals increased their utilization by about 85 percent over the period.

If we apply this increased utilization factor for short-term hospitals to total hospital expenditures over the quarter century, the base figure of $3.7 billion in 1950 would rise to $7.12 billion in 1974. Making a second correction for the declining value of the dollar will bring the latter total to $11.3 billion. With total hospital expenditures of $43.5 billion in 1974, an increase of over $32 billion still remains to be explained. Accounting for this huge sum will not be easy.

In many segments of the economy, an increase in the level of output facilitates economies in the use of labor and other resources; this is not the case in the area of hospital care. From 1950 to 1973, personnel per 100 patients increased from 84 to 233 overall; and in short-term hospitals, from 178 to 315.[37] Thus the number of people employed to care for the same number of patients in short-term hospitals increased by 77 percent over the period. This is one major source of the cost escalation. One way to interpret this large increase of personnel per patient would be to look for changes in the intensity of services rendered that required more staff time. But other interpretations must also be explored.

The marked increase in personnel appears to be associated with a reduction, not an increase, in the amount of personal attention that the average patient received. At the same time that personnel-to-patient ratios were rising, workers negotiated shorter hours, more paid holidays, longer annual vacations, and regular coffee breaks, so the effective number of working hours per employee were reduced. These reductions in total hours did not, however, cancel out the increase in the total personnel complement. How then can we account for the widespread impression of many observers that the expanded staff resulted in less attention to the individual patient? There are several possible explanations. Patients who are seriously ill receive more attention, for recovery rooms and the intensive care units are heavily staffed. Next, hospitals added large numbers of half-trained and untrained workers whose productivity is relatively low and who, as noted earlier, require close supervision. A former Commissioner of Hospitals of New York City once commented that his small cadre of registered nurses were so busy making sure that their assistants were following instructions that they had no time to do any nursing, even for the seriously ill patients who required special attention.

In the quarter century following the end of World War II, the total number of hospital personnel increased from slightly over 1 million to about 2.8 million, and the wages per employee also increased substantially.[37] For many years students of hospital economics estimated that labor costs represented at least two-thirds of all hospital expenditures, and that the remainder went to nonlabor inputs, such as fuel, food, and pharmaceuticals. Recent studies by Victor Fuchs and others have indicated a decline in the last decade in the proportion of labor costs to total expenditures of about 10 percentage points.[38] Their explanation is that the growing sophistication of medical technology has led hospitals to increase their outlays for the purchase and maintenance of new equipment. There has also been greater use of consumables, from X-ray film to drugs. And more recently, the steep rise in the prices of heating, lighting, and other basic operating requirements has also contributed to the rise in nonlabor costs.

Further perspective is offered by Martin Feldstein, who has pointed out that, as late as 1960, hospital employees received between 20 to 30 percent less than employees in comparable occupations in other industries.[39] But a decade later a substantial correction had taken place. By then hospital workers had the edge over other workers in many comparable occupations, an advantage they kept during the first half of the 1970s. This wage correction, which took place within relatively few years, may have added as much as $6 billion to the hospital wage bill by the mid-1970s.

Since the early days of modern medical education, major teaching hospitals have done more than just provide an advanced level of care to certain patients. They have also played an ever larger role in the undergraduate and graduate education of the larger student bodies and have become the focal centers for more and more of the nation's intensified research efforts. After World War II, new funding became available for research primarily from the expanded National Institutes of Health, and after the middle 1960s, new monies were also made available for the expansion of the hospitals' educational mission through construction, program, and capitation grants. The result was greater commingling of patient care with education and research. Although attempts have been made to sort out the cost of each of these three functions—patient care, education, and research—in large teaching hospitals, neither the economists nor the accountants have made much headway. The reason is that when all three functions are performed in one institution, there is a transformation of the total product. While a small hospital with neither a teaching nor a research program can care for a range of patients requiring medical or surgical care, only the large teaching institution is in a position to provide complex types of care such as a coronary by-pass or a kidney transplant.

Until now it has been impossible to sort out the cost of patient care from the educational and research functions performed by large teaching hospitals; we can nevertheless identify some of the more important reasons for their much higher per diem costs. We have already noted that these large centers tend to admit a disproportionate share of patients who require more complex types of treatment and who therefore carry a substantially higher daily cost since they involve more diagnostic, surgical, and postoperative care. Such patients require more staff to care for them, and they are likely to undergo elaborate tests and other diagnostic procedures. Instead of being in the operating room for thirty minutes, they may be there for three hours; they are likely to require a longer stay in the recovery room and may have to spend several days in the intensive care unit.

Faced with a patient whose condition requires the use of complex and often risky procedures, the physician in charge is likely to proceed methodically in assessing each successive stage, for he is also teaching medical students to determine the optimal method of treatment. This correlative teaching function will almost certainly lead him along a decision path that adds considerably to the total costs. If the patient can be included in a current research effort, he is likely to have additional services prescribed that derive almost exclusively from the research effort and that may have little effect on his treatment or recovery.

Most of our large teaching hospitals have multiple sources of funding, which is one reason why third-party payors are distressed by their inability to acquire effective understanding of, much less control over, hospital cost structures. But these shortcomings must not obscure the fact that up to now the funds required to operate these dynamic institutions with their interrelated functions have been forthcoming. This, in itself, is important, since it suggests that the public has been willing to make the necessary resources available to assure their growth and development. But it does not answer the basic problem, which is that no adequate mechanism exists for balancing the social benefits and costs resulting from these constantly increasing inputs of funds.

The essence of a dynamic economy is that it creates an incentive for the innovative entrepreneur to forecast the types of new goods and services that the public desires and to provide them before his competitors do. In the private sector, new goods and services are subject to constant check by the willingness of consumers to pay a price for the new product that will cover all of the costs and leave some profit for expansion. It could be argued that this happened in the expansion of hospital care and the financing that supported it. If the funds had not been forthcoming, the expansion could not have taken place. But this interpretation, although formally correct, obscures a great deal. During the last quarter century, there has been a vast alteration in the basis of financing hospital care, and an appraisal of this transformation is necessary in order to understand what happened.

In 1950 the two principal sources of funding—private and public—contributed approximately equal shares to total hospital expenditures. Within the private sector, direct payments by patients accounted for just under two-thirds of all payments, and insurance companies accounted for less than one-third. By 1975, after a more than twelvefold increase in total expenditures for hospital care—from under $4 billion to about $48 billion annually—the sources of funding had altered radically. First, the ratio of public to private financing had shifted modestly from approximately 46:54 to 55:45. A more striking transformation occurred within the private sector. Here direct payments by patients for hospital care declined to about 10 percent, with a corresponding increase in insurance benefits to 75 percent.[9]

The single most critical change during these years affected the mechanism of payment for hospital care. In 1950 only 17 percent of all expenditures for hospital care were covered by insurance. By 1975, private insurance and government insurance (primarily Medicare) covered all but a minimum of these expenditures. Direct consumer payments had shrunk to 10 percent.[9]

As long as hospitals sought payment directly from the patient for 2 out of every 3 dollars billed, they had to be concerned with the ability of the patient to meet their charges. They knew that some patients would be unable to pay, that others could pay only part, and that government or philanthropy would have to cover the remainder. However, consideration of the consumer's ability to pay became less important once insurance and government became the primary sources of payment, especially during the years when they reimbursed hospitals for their costs without critical review.

There is a strong presumption that the easing of the payment problem contributed substantially to the escalation of hospital costs. Hospital trustees, the director, and the staff found the setting favorable to expansion. Since the hospital would be reimbursed for whatever it spent, the administration did not hesitate to undertake expensive new expansions, especially since the prestige of the institution depended upon the growth and diversification of its functions. However, before we can conclude that cost escalation was attributable to the alteration in the payment mechanism, we should look at trends in the three other large components of health care expenditures—dentistry, drugs, and nursing home care.

Of the $12 billion total expenditure for health in 1950, dentistry accounted for about $1 billion and drugs for $1.64 billion. Expenditures for nursing home care were less than $200 million. Comparable 1975 outlays were $7.8 billion for dentistry, $10.3 billion for drugs, and $9.1 billion for nursing home care out of a total of $122.2 billion.[9]

Several facts stand out. Dentistry and drugs together declined from 21 percent of total expenditures to about 15 percent. On the other hand, expenditures for nursing home care increased to a point where this category ranked fourth in order of all recent expenditures for health care. Trends in the outlays for dental services paralleled those for physician services. The primary cause of the steep rise in total expenditures was institutional care in hospitals and nursing homes.

If we attempt to relate these trends to payment mechanisms, we find that in 1974 approximately five-sixths of all expenditures for both dentistry and drugs represented direct payments by the consumer.[9] Does this mean that direct payment generates a slower rate of growth? Not really, since the increase in expenditures for dental services was similar to that for medical services, although the consumer paid directly for five-sixths of the former and for only one-third of the latter.

With regard to nursing home care, it should be noted that governmental payments account for about 55 percent of the total, and that private insurance companies pay for only a minor share. Although private entrepreneurship has taken the lead in expanding nursing home care facilities and now accounts for 16,000 of the 21,000 nursing homes, over half of all payments for care in these nursing homes is covered by public funds.[37]

We find, then, that with the single exception of dentistry, expenditures grew most rapidly in those sectors where direct consumer payments were increasingly replaced by public funds or by insurance. But that may be too fine a distinction:

expenditures for every major component of the health care industry, except drugs, grew rapidly during the last quarter century, and in every area other than drugs and dentistry third-party payments now predominate.

One might ask why there is such excitement about rising costs. In one way or another the consumer covers the bill—either through direct payments, insurance premiums, or taxes. Further, there is no evidence that he has yet reached a point of resistance to this steeply rising bill. However, we have earlier noted signs of a rougher road ahead. The federal and state governments have sought to cut back the scale of entitlements for various types of health care that they pay for, and private and nonprofit insurance companies are increasingly constrained by superintendents of insurance not to raise their premiums by the full amount required to cover burgeoning hospital costs. Steeply rising malpractice insurance rates now contribute to further escalation of costs. But the real challenge comes from the growing public awareness that the entire health care system is out of control, with neither the consumer, nor the insurance underwriters, nor the government able to restrain the upward drift in costs.

Estimates prepared by the Congressional Budget Office in 1976 projected the following increases over the next five years in the federal budget alone if existing programs are maintained. Taking into account both direct expenditures and tax benefits (these are the result of subsidies to employees and individuals for health care expenditures that amounted to $6.6 billion in 1976), the total current federal outlays of $50 billion are projected to rise to approximately $80 billion, or by some 60 percent, within five years. [40] Whereas about one-fifth of this increase will be needed to cover additional beneficiaries, primarily for Medicare, the remaining 80 percent reflects higher medical costs. It should be stressed that these projections do not include either funding for new programs or liberalization of existing programs. However, if the past provides any clue to the future, it is highly unlikely that the federal government will not respond to any of the multiple pressures constantly impinging upon it to increase its outlays in one or another aspect of the health industry, including manpower, facilities, research, and services.

The Congressional Budget Office (CBO) analysis points out that this projected $80 billion for 1981 might be lowered by about $9 billion if the federal government were to increase co-insurance payments by Medicare patients; limit reimbursement for providers, primarily hospitals; and reduce matching funds to the states for Medicaid. But the CBO also describes three "higher options" and calculates their respective costs. A program that would provide comprehensive coverage for the entire low-income population and protection against catastrophic expenses for all citizens would entail an additional expenditure of between $20 to $25 billion annually. A comprehensive health insurance system financed by premium payments would require additional expenditures of between $23 and $34 billion. Finally, a tax-financed comprehensive insurance system would entail some $100 to $130 billion of additional expenditure. If the last were adopted, federal expenditures in 1981 could approximate $200 billion and total national expenditures could approach the $300 billion level.[40] Since aggregate national expenditures for health in Fiscal Year 1976 have been calculated at $139 billion, a possible doubling of this sum within five years is cause for deliberation, perhaps anxiety.

Much of the cost increase over the past decade has been generated by efforts to increase equity in access to health care. This consideration continues to play a part in our efforts to shape future reforms, from programs providing increased protection against catastrophic costs to the conversion of health care into a fully tax-supported system. The next chapter will explore the potentials and limitations of moving toward equity in a democratic society that is characterized by vast differences in personal income and regional health resources.

8

Equity

THE PRECEDING discussions of access, quality, and costs have all touched on the question of equity. Clearly, equity is the implicit criterion by which we assess whether and to what extent different groups in a society have access to preventive, therapeutic, and rehabilitative services. Most people today would consider it unconscionable for an affluent society to regulate the access of its citizens to life-preserving and pain-relieving services on the basis of their inherited wealth or earned income. Such a market-determined approach is abhorrent when young children and older persons are considered. Members of religious orders, impelled by the belief that no society, regardless of its material circumstances, may turn its back on those in need at a time of illness, have historically ministered to the health needs of the poor. Although there was often little that treatment could accomplish, they held it a moral imperative to demonstrate concern and to provide support to the sick and injured.

In an advanced industrial society with a sophisticated health system, the relation between equity and access to medical care revolves around elimination of the financial barrier. Early proponents of social reform, even in the days of Count Bismarck, recognized that the random incidence of severe illness and injury could make it difficult even for the average citizen, let alone those at the lower end of the income distribution, to meet the costs of treatment solely through personal savings. Since a family with moderate or low income could not be expected to cover its high costs for medical care out of past savings or current earnings, insurance offered the only feasible alternative. Under a comprehensive system of insurance, every member of the society would be assured access to care in time of need, and sufficient revenues could be raised from the population at large to meet the total costs of the system. By placing the financing of health care within the framework of social insurance, it would be possible to raise the needed resources through a combination of premium payments and tax revenues. In light of the progressive structure of the income tax, the higher the proportion of revenues raised through taxes, the greater the relative contribution of the affluent.

Over the last century, most of the countries of Western Europe as well as Canada and other British dominions have resorted to a system of social insurance for health care. With the enactment of the National Health Service in 1948, the United Kingdom went the farthest both in providing comprehensive services and in radically limiting the potential of the private sector to compete with the public system. The United States has moved the shortest distance toward social insurance, and currently uses the mechanism of social insurance solely for Medicare. Currently, the aggregate contribution of all levels of government—federal, state, and local—covers about 40 percent of the total health expenditures of the American people.[9]

Opinions differ among students of the American health care system about how far we have succeeded in reducing the financial barriers to health care. The critics emphasize that a significant proportion of the population, highly concentrated among those at the lower end of the income distribution, do not have insurance coverage for hospital costs or for other medical needs. According to the *Economic Report of the President* (1976), in 1970 voluntary insurance covered only 23 percent of inpatient expenditures of families of four with incomes of $5,700 or less. For families above this income level, voluntary insurance covered 53 percent of all hospital expenditures and physicians' fees. It is further charged—and correctly—that only a small percentage of all low-income families are insured for comprehensive services. Critics of the system also point out that, even with Medicare, only slightly more than 40 percent of the total health expenditures of older persons is covered (largely because Medicare does not cover long-term care). The rest must be paid from income, savings, contributions from other members of the family, or covered by Medicaid.

According to a report to the Senate and House Committees on the Budget (*Budget Options for Fiscal Year 1978*), prepared by the Congressional Budget Office in February 1977, "Approximately 40 million people with incomes under $10,000 have inadequate health insurance protection and are ineligible for Medicaid." An estimated 25 million people (about 12 percent of the population) have neither private nor public coverage. Most of these people are self-employed, unemployed, chronically ill, students, or employees of small low-wage businesses. Some 8 million of these uninsured persons may be able to obtain services from a source such as the Veterans Administration, but that still leaves 17 million who must bear the full financial burden of their health care.

A first tentative conclusion from the foregoing must be that whatever progress toward equity the United States has made in the past years, we are still far from the goal of removing the financial barrier to health care for the entire population. On the other hand, it is essential that we take a closer look at recent developments in order to see the extent to which previously existing differentials in access to care, based on financial considerations, have been narrowed.

Although there are little reliable data about the utilization of health services by different income groups over the last several decades, a synthesis of cross-sectional analyses demonstrates unequivocally that, as a result of its greatly increased health expenditures, the nation has achieved a substantial narrowing of differential rates of utilization by income class of both outpatient and inpatient services.

But since the poor are likely to need additional services because of their higher rate of disability, even an equalization of service use may not reflect the complete elimination of financial barriers. And if we look beyond routine visits to physicians and hospitalization and consider preventive and rehabilitative services, a significant utilization differential remains. The poor are less likely to receive an annual physical examination, to have an eye examination and to purchase eyeglasses. And in the event of a serious disability resulting from trauma or stroke, they are less likely to have access to rehabilitative services that could restore partial or complete functioning. The general conclusion in the *Economic Report of the President* that "even taking into account differences in sickness, overall access to treatment seems fairly equalized," exaggerates the extent to which equality of access has been achieved.

Nowhere is this easier to demonstrate than with respect to the utilization of dental services, which remains more highly income-related than any other type of health service including psychiatry. Individuals in higher-income classes start to visit a dentist in their youth, are likely to have orthodontic appliances, and continue to seek dental treatment on a preventive basis throughout their adult life. Children of low-income families seldom see a dentist and almost never see an orthodontist. As adults, they go to a dentist primarily for the extraction of an aching tooth and are much more likely to lose all or most of their teeth by the age of fifty or sixty.

But the example of dental care also points to the need to consider other factors besides income that influence utilization. As we saw in Chapter 5, aside from financial resources, the two most important determinants of the demand for health care are education and style of life. The conditions for which and under which people seek health care depend in some measure on their understanding of the capabilities and limitations of modern medicine. Individuals with little education who are uninformed about advances in the treatment of disease are less likely to seek health care either for themselves or for the members of their family. Certain types of therapy, such as psychoanalysis, may be precluded by the lack of an adequate educational base. A certain level of general sophistication, itself linked to the level of formal education, is required before a patient can relate symptoms and actions to prior conditions and experiences. In addition, the poorly educated are less likely to seek help at the first appearance of a symptom that may portend serious trouble.

Attitudes, values, and life styles also affect the demand for medical care. We have noted that there are minorities in this country—Christian Scientists, for example—who refuse to seek help from health professionals. Others hold views and follow practices that limit their recourse to the health care system. These include individuals who believe implicitly in the efficacy of diet or are confirmed adherents of chiropractic or other nontraditional therapies. And large numbers prefer to rely primarily on self-ministrations.

Thus even the total elimination of the financial barrier—an ideal that probably cannot be achieved in any complex society—would not in and of itself assure equality in the use of health services. In the developed countries, financial resources no longer influence the distribution of health services as significantly as they did in the past. Education and life style also help to perpetuate a differential utilization of health care.

Societies become so fixed in their ways of thinking and acting that they often continue to define issues in traditional terms that are no longer appropriate. We have acknowledged that income still affects the distribution of health services, but it may be more useful to shift our analysis from inequalities in access to care to inequalities in the types of care received. Individuals in the lower-income groups are more likely to be handicapped by the inferior quality of the services to which they have access than to be blocked from access entirely.

The difficulties that the poor experience in obtaining an acceptable level of health care in a large metropolis are easily enumerated. Most of the urban poor turn for basic medical care to the emergency room or outpatient department of a large hospital. In such a setting they characteristically see a different physician on each visit. Since patient records are not readily retrievable and often lack essential entries, each patient encounter requires that the physician start anew to acquaint himself with the patient's medical history and current symptomatology. And since effective therapy often requires the patient's adherence to a drug or other regimen, the lack of a continuing doctor-patient relationship militates against the patient's compliance. Moreover, the outpatient departments of most large teaching hospitals are organized by specialty or subspecialty. This means that the patient with multiple problems is treated by several physicians who only rarely consult with each other to decide on an optimal overall therapeutic plan.

Contrast this with the conditions under which a person in a middle-income family receives care from his family physician. Two major differences are immediately apparent. His physician knows him, has treated his family, and has a record of his earlier diseases. This provides a much firmer basis for treating the patient's current illness. Moreover, the physician in private practice is under subtle pressure early on to relate to his patient so as to gain and hold his confidence; otherwise, he risks losing that patient, other members of his family, and even relatives and friends. No practitioner can afford to be brusque, uninterested, or discourteous to those who pay him. Although many clinic physicians treat the poor with consideration and courtesy, they are under less pressure to do so and we know from patient reports that many do not.

When the urban poor look to other community health resources than the hospital for outpatient care, they are likely to confront several alternatives. There may be a few private practitioners in their neighborhood. These are primarily older physicians who have no hospital affiliation, have not participated in continuing education, and spend little time reading the medical journals or attending professional meetings to keep themselves abreast of new developments. Their office equipment is likely to be old and often in need of repairs. Some of these inner-city practitioners are foreign medical graduates who have failed to complete their residency in the U.S. and may not be licensed. Many have language difficulties in communicating with their patients.

The urban poor can also obtain ambulatory care in neighborhood health centers or medical groups that have been organized specifically to treat a large Medicaid clientele. In the former instance, the center may be loosely organized and staffed, with casual linkages to a supporting hospital for the referral of patients with difficult diagnoses or complicated therapeutic requirements. Effective linkages between clinic and hospital staffs are not easy to establish and maintain and, in time, a neighborhood health center is as likely to lose its original dynamic leadership and decline as it is to grow and improve. On the other hand, some of the private medical groups that have located in low-income neighborhoods are primarily interested in high profits, and their style of practice reflects this. Most patients are seen and treated in a cursory fashion. Many are encouraged to return for additional visits whether these are medically indicated or not. They are advised to submit to a wide range of tests for conditions that are unrelated to their complaints and are urged to buy drugs or medical supplies from sources that have a business relation with the group.

Federal, state, and local governmental inspectors as well as investigative reporters have exposed an increasing number of Medicaid scandals. Many of the revelations have focused on outright fraud—practitioners requesting reimbursement for treatments not rendered. But the greater shortcoming of the system as revealed by these exposés is the poor quality of the care that many in the low-income group receive. One of the more distressing findings is the unwillingness of many of the Medicaid mills to treat patients whose conditions require special effort. These patients are often turned away with the suggestion that they seek treatment elsewhere. Clearly, government must become better informed about the services it pays for via Medicaid. From the occasional reports that have been made public, there is reason to believe that much of the ambulatory care provided the poor by these Medicaid mills is at best ineffective and at worst results in the neglect or improper treatment of serious health conditions.

The quality of inpatient care also differs for the poor and the affluent. To begin with, the poor patient is less likely to be admitted to a large teaching hospital unless his condition is interesting to those concerned with teaching or research. He is also less likely to be admitted by a physician who is familiar with his medical history and who assumes responsibility for the care that he will receive. In hospitals that treat predominantly poor patients, the nursing and other services are frequently understaffed and specialized equipment is either unavailable or poorly maintained. The poor are cared for by a house staff that is seldom equal to the staffs of hospitals that cater to middle-class patients. Moreover, the attending physicians in hospitals that admit large numbers of poor people are less directly concerned with supervision of the house staff; they leave that to the senior resident. Clearly, a poor person admitted to a hospital in which the predominant patient load consists of inner-city residents will not receive the same level of care as that provided to affluent patients admitted to a major teaching hospital.

Although the presumption of gross differences in the quality of care that different groups of patients receive has been acknowledged by informed persons, few systematic studies have been made of how patient diagnosis, level of care provided, and outcome differ among hospitals that operate under different auspices and that admit patients from different income groups.

It is even more difficult to document that differences in the quality of care exert a significant impact on outcomes. Unless there is gross neglect, egregious error, or extreme incompetence, most patients survive a medical encounter. They may not profit from treatment, but most of them will escape serious adverse effects. This difficulty of linking quality of care directly to outcome helps to explain why discussions of equity so frequently fail to consider the quality dimension.

In addition to access and quality, there is a third aspect of equity, which we can designate as equity in paying for the costs of care. We have noted that most advanced industrial nations have adopted social insurance as the preferred mechanism of paying for health care on the assumption that a combination of wage deductions and tax revenues derived from a progressive income tax levy best distributes the burden of payment between high- and low-income groups. In the United States, where a more diversified payment pattern prevails and we have come to rely increasingly on private insurance and public subsidy, there are many misconceptions about the true burden of meeting health care costs. One way to dramatize the difference between popular opinion and the realities of finance is to compare the conventional beliefs with those of the experts.

—*Public opinion* believes that the use of the Social Security system, which derives its revenues from taxes paid by both employees and employers as well as from a contribution out of general revenues, represents a major step toward the achievement of equity. But this assessment comes up against two important facts: the regressiveness of the Social Security tax and the fact that as of 1976 Medicare covered only 42 percent of the total health expenditures of the enrolled population.

—*Public opinion* believes that the rise in government's (federal, state, and local) share of health care financing from 25 percent to over 40 percent in the last two decades is a step in the direction of equity and does in fact represent a form of transfer payment to the poor and the near poor. But the fact is that a substantial share of this enlarged governmental outlay falls on the average taxpayer: families earning between $10,000 and $20,000 annually.

—*Public opinion* and the advocates of tax-funded national health insurance argue that the costs of health care would be met by those most able to pay, thereby making the financial burden more equitably shared than at present. But the only safe assumption of the various alternative designs for a tax-funded plan, as reported by a 1976 Rand study, is that the new taxes will fall on the same groups in approximately the same proportions as current taxes.[41] This means that most of the costs of the new plan will continue to fall on the large middle group of taxpayers.

The implication of this is simple but critical. A high-income society is able to alter the pattern of payment for medical care by shifting the amounts contributed respectively by employers, in the form of fringe benefits or social security taxes; by employees, through contributions to joint management-labor plans or through social security taxes; by taxpayers, via general revenues; and by consumers, through insurance premiums or fee-for-service payments. Alternative patterns ease some of the burden for payment on those at the low end of the income scale by extracting some additional monies from those who are at the top. Nevertheless, there is no way in which the large group of taxpayers in the middle can avoid carrying most of the costs of health care or any other large governmental program.

In a democracy there is little or no prospect of fundamentally altering the pattern of payment for a service that commands more than 10 percent of the nation's disposable income without a radical change in existing power and property relations. The very poor may receive an assist and the wealthy may be forced to pay something extra, but there is no way for a government to provide significantly more services to the citizenry unless the majority of the taxpayers pay for what they receive.

For proof of the restricted margin that exists for large-scale redistribution of health services, we need only recall the history of Medicaid. Very soon after its enactment, the federal government and many of the states found it necessary to curtail the relatively liberal entitlements and the relatively broad range of services that they had initially underwritten. A similar review of recent Medicare experience points to the repeated efforts by the Administration, sometimes with the support of Congress, sometimes without, to control the public's commitments by raising the coinsurance requirements for beneficiaries and by restricting the scope of services.

There is a further relation between personal income and equity in health care that warrants at least brief attention. Many patients suffer chronic conditions, such as heart disease or diabetes, whose effective treatment requires, in addition to competent medical care, adjustments in life style—changes in occupation, living quarters, diet. However, the disabled member of a low-income family has much less scope for making these adjustments than the affluent individual. A poor man must often continue to work full-time; he is unable to find an apartment within his means that does not necessitate his climbing four flights of stairs; his budget may not permit him to substitute suitable foods for those that should be eliminated from his diet. Since the restoration of a patient to an effective level of functioning often requires costly adjustments in his style of life, the well-to-do are in a better position than the poor to effect these changes.

Two additional facets of equity remain to be identified and briefly assessed. The first relates the issue of equity to the distribution of health resources. The second involves the quantity and quality of health resources allocated to groups with differing conditions and complaints.

Many countries have gone far toward equalizing access to care by removing financial barriers, without altering the distribution of health manpower and facilities. In the U.S.S.R. there are special institutions to provide medical care for the governmental and scientific elite and the members of their families. In Sweden even an emergency admission to a hospital of one's choice may depend on personal relations with the chief of the service. In Rumania a physician will visit patients in their home only if he receives a sizable fee "under the table." The story is told of a prominent member of the Israeli establishment who was on a waiting list for two years for a herniorrhaphy at the Hebrew University-Hadassah Medical Center; he was placed at the head of the queue only after his election to the presidency of Israel because his hernia was then viewed as an occupational hazard.

In the United States persons enrolled in prepayment plans often must wait for some period of time before they can see a consultant, receive certain tests, or be admitted to a hospital. Although in general a patient does not object to a short waiting period for elective surgery, the inadequacy of resources frequently results in waiting periods that are considered excessive by professionals and consumers alike. Without an abundance of all types of health resources, a situation socially costly to develop and maintain, some form of rationing is unavoidable.

The final issue related to equity is difficult to assess and more difficult to integrate within the society's decision-making process. It relates to the fact that different groups in the society present different health problems and that there is no easy way—in fact, no way other than political decision-making—to determine the relative claims of these several groups on health resources.

Several recent American and foreign developments help to illuminate the most complex dimension of equity—ordering the claims of persons with different types of disability. In the United States the decision to add renal dialysis treatments to health care covered by Medicare was a decision reached during Congressional debate in 1972 without formal committee hearings or staff review of the costs that such an additional benefit was likely to entail. In 1976 these costs approximated $300 million annually and, unless there is a radical technological breakthrough, are likely to climb within the next few years to the billion-dollar level.[42]

A recent report (early 1977) on coronary by-pass surgery suggests that many patients suffering from angina pectoris will do as well on drug therapy. Since the surgical procedure costs between $7,000 and $10,000, an alternative therapy is an important matter to the public authorities who cover most of the costs of care for Medicare patients.

During the 1960s the infant mortality rate in the United States appeared to have reached a plateau at a level half again as high as prevails in the leading advanced nations.[18] From this observation, many critics of the U.S. health care system jumped to the conclusion that only a marked improvement in maternal and child care services—prenatal, delivery, and postnatal—held out any promise for renewed decline in this critical indicator. Although Medicaid did make additional health care services available to the poor, among whom the infant mortality rates were far above the national average, no large-scale program aimed at improved services for pregnant women was instituted. The only exception was the legalization of abortion on demand.

Lately, after several years of stability, the infant mortality rate again started to decline and has continued on its downward path. The reasons for its earlier stabilization as well as its renewed decline appear to be linked only indirectly to the changing pattern of health care delivery. The socio-environmental determinants, such as education, income, and socialization, are probably the crucial factors.

We noted earlier that long-term care for older persons is not provided for under Medicare. A total of 100 days of such care is all that can be reimbursed, and then only if a patient is transferred to a nursing home after a minimum of three days of hospitalization.

During the last years, many states have begun to empty their mental hospitals. But few of these states have been able to make available the range of supportive services in the community that would ensure proper care for those discharged from mental hospitals. The fact that many who are discharged return to the hospital within a few months or a year indicates that either they were not ready for discharge or that they did not receive essential support on the outside, or both.

It is not easy to rank the claims of different groups of patients with respect to long-term care, by-pass surgery, renal dialysis, maternal and child care, and mental care. And there surely is no easy way to determine where equity lies. To say that a society should meet quickly all of these needs is not an effective answer. Such a proposal could be taken seriously only to the extent that the financing and other resources required to turn the commitment into reality were carefully detailed and could win the citizenry's approval.

It is worth pointing out that recent criticisms of the National Health Service in Great Britain have revealed substantial neglect of the needs of mental and chronic patients. Clearly, in a world of limited resources, the existence of a national plan to finance and deliver health services to the population is no assurance that different groups of claimants will be treated equitably. There is ample room in a democracy for discriminating in favor of one group to the disadvantage of other groups, and this is apparently what has happened in Great Britain during the past several decades with respect to mental and chronic patients.

Recent Canadian health planning has formulated a broad-scale attack on the linkages between resources and effectiveness that underlie the issue of equity. It is argued that most of the nation's health resources are directed to services whose utilization will have little effect upon the longevity or the morbidity of the recipients. In the view of the health planners, a true advance in health status would require a radical redirection of resources toward the reduction and ultimate elimination of the pathogenic forces in the environment and in the living patterns of the public. Only then would health dollars be well spent; only then would the population at large benefit.

Attempting to shift the focus of health care from an ever increasing allocation of resources for therapeutic purposes to an increased emphasis on prevention that can be tied to improved health status is appealing and hard-headed. But this shift is easier to develop on paper than in life. There is no agreement among the experts about what preventive measures now available in the arsenal of modern medicine are currently being neglected. They agree that people eat too much, drive too fast, drink too much, exercise too little. But there is no easy way—possibly no way at all—for society to bring about a significant change in the population's behavior.

And the same is true about improvements in the environment, where admittedly many pathogens have their origin. Once again, we know more about what we should avoid—the use of carcinogenic substances, air and water pollution, dangerous working conditions—than how to protect ourselves from these hazards. There is no way to make the environment totally safe, and the cost of making it a little safer can often prove excessive.

Clearly equity, access, and quality remain elusive goals. How a society can steal up on them, even if it cannot capture and control them, is the concern of the remaining chapters.

Part Three

Prospects for Reform

9

Priorities

A CONSTANT TENSION is built into the process of political reform in a democracy. What usually happens is that some advocacy groups identify a significant weakness in the performance of the economy or society and formulate goals that, if pursued, in their opinion will remedy the deficiency. But there is always a second group—for shorthand purposes we can define them as conservatives—who, without necessarily denying various shortcomings, inefficiencies, and inequities, oppose changing the status quo. Their opposition to change, particularly to radical change, stems from their concern about the resources required to alter the extant system and from doubts as to whether the desired outcomes could be realized even if changes were made.

For years a tension between reformers and conservatives has characterized the arena of health reform in the United States. It permeates the present public debate about what should be done to alter the present system, at what rate the reforms should be introduced, and what the reasonable expectations are that the changes will succeed in eliminating the most important deficits.

This chapter will address the issue of priority reforms that are currently being pursued and seek to identify some of the constraints that will determine whether and to what extent the proposed reforms are likely to be enacted. It will also evaluate whether the reforms, if enacted, are likely to fulfill the expectations of their proponents.

One pervasive difficulty in dealing with prescriptions for social action—that is, every reform effort—should be made explicit. It is the old ends-means dilemma, the tendency to confuse the outcomes sought with the instruments to be used. Reform of the health care system is a matter of great concern because the public has ascribed to it the potential for reducing morbidity, increasing longevity, alleviating pain and anxiety, improving productivity, and in numerous other ways enhancing the quality of human life.

The priority issues that are at the center of the debate on health reform center around the early introduction of national health insurance, greater governmental involvement in the education and distribution of physicians, new societal arrangements to control the continuing escalation in costs, a better delivery system, and an improved planning mechanism to narrow the gap between unmet needs and available, or potentially available, resources capable of meeting these needs.

The American people believe that the manner in which they respond to these issues—the actions they will take as well as those they will avoid—will have a material effect on the prolongation of life, the reduction of disease, and the relief of pain and anxiety, which are the real goals they seek from the health care system.

No society, and surely not one as complex and specialized as ours, can move directly toward the realization of important goals. Action can take place only through the selection and use of one group of instrumentalities and techniques in preference to another—if necessary creating new instruments and techniques.

Every effort at social reform involves, therefore, a reconciliation of the ends-means dilemma. It is often easier to achieve consensus about the goals of social reform than about the means to be employed to pursue specific targets. In the current debate over health reform, many protagonists are paying close attention to the distribution of physicians per 100,000 population in different areas, the changing trend in the number of patient-physician encounters, and the proportion of the population who are members of prepaid health plans. In their concern with these and other indices, the debaters are often unaware that the goals of improved health and the measures used to assess health are not the same. It may be inevitable that all efforts at social reform slip from ends to means, but we must attempt to distinguish between the two.

A parallel formulation is the need to differentiate process from outcome variables. A process variable is the number of times a patient sees his physician; the outcome variable is whether, as a result of the visit, the patient is freed from his disability and can function better.

Another difficulty is always present where reforms are concerned. Individuals and societies never pursue a single goal, not even in time of war when survival is imperative. Consequently, the costs of progressing toward any specific goal, such as improved health, must include not only an estimate of the additional resources required but also a judgment about whether other important values may be jeopardized or lost if the priority goal is aggressively pursued.

Human beings are not automatons. Patient and physician act and react in response to a wide range of stimuli, and the effectiveness with which a health system operates cannot be dissociated from the forces that influence the behavior of each. Not even a police state has as yet forced its members to take better care of their health. True, the U.S. Army in World War II disciplined soldiers who contracted frostbite, on the theory that if they had followed instructions they would not have become disabled. And the Russians are said to have instituted such a stringent regimen at some of their sanatoria that no worker who has been released would willingly return. But when individuals do not pose a threat to others, even highly organized societies are disinclined to use the power of the state to control their behavior, even when their behavior is likely to be deleterious to their health. We are a long way from fining people who are seriously overweight, who fail to follow the regimen prescribed by their physician, who fail to exercise an hour a day.

The process of health reform is further confused by the need to distinguish between the availability of resources and their effective utilization, which requires appropriate behavior on the part of both providers and consumers. Short of incontrovertible evidence of malpractice, there is no way to impose external controls upon the practitioner to assure that he is conscientious in his diagnosis and treatment. And it is well known that a patient frequently reports to his physician that he is complying with the prescribed course of medication without having done so, or even intending to do so.

There is no need to expand this discussion of the many discrepancies between the pursuit of health goals and the instruments used to effect their realization. The argument is simple and direct: mechanisms cannot be equated with outcomes. This does not imply that reforms are unachievable or that, if achieved, they will necessarily fall short of their promise. Rather, they are designed to inject a note of realism into

the subject. As Richard Crossman has pointed out in his illuminating *Diary of a Cabinet Minister,* it is in the nature of
politics for government leaders to deal with a few singular
propositions.[43] Health care, however, is a complex system,
and its shortcomings cannot be cured by any one nostrum,
even one as powerful as a national health service.

As the decade of the 1970s draws to a close, the United
States approaches the problem of health reform along two in-
tersecting axes. The first is a composite of changes that is
directed to enlarging the output of desired health services,
from prevention to rehabilitation, and to improving their distribution. The second is more specifically focused on organizational, manpower, and administrative rearrangements
aimed at assuring that the costs of reforms are reasonably contained and that they are shared equitably among the citizenry.

As is always the case in an evolutionary rather than a revolutionary era, many of the building blocks out of which reforms
must be shaped are already at hand. The first is the range of instruments that can be used to slow the spiraling of costs, particularly hospital costs, by introducing one or another alternative
to the established practice of reimbursing institutions on the
basis of their past costs.

The second building block involves new approaches aimed
at modifying the uncontrolled outcomes of financial and institutional decision-making whereby the graduates of medical
schools have been free to choose their area of specialization
within the alternatives offered by the training system. Moreover, when their training is completed, they are free to decide
where to practice. Recently, with the federal government in
the lead followed by state governments, these relatively free-
market structures have been—and continue to be—ma-
nipulated through a combination of legislative, financial,
and administrative arrangements to influence the distribution

of physicians with respect to both their specialization and location.

Another new departure has been the special efforts of the federal government, certain large private insurance companies, and various consumer groups to experiment with new forms of health delivery systems. The protagonists are convinced that until there are many more functioning alternatives to the conventional fee-for-service system of care, there is little prospect of providing comprehensive health services at a cost that the citizen-consumer can pay.

The realization that history, and history alone, has been responsible for the complex structures that characterize the health care systems of different communities, and the further realization that the extant system frequently fails to provide for even the essential needs of some groups, has led the federal government to press for an intensified planning approach to health reform. It is expected that through cooperative efforts at area, state, and federal levels, it will be possible to coordinate the existing resources of the health care system with the priority needs of the American people. The planning approach represents another departure.

The final approach that requires careful assessment is national health insurance, as presented in one or another of the major proposals that have been formulated to provide basic coverage for meeting the essential health needs of the entire population.

The present strategy for slowing the steeply rising trend of health care expenditures seeks to control the increase of facilities and expensive new equipment; to prevent providers, particularly hospitals, from passing all of their expenditures on to government and insurance plans for full reimbursement; to shift the production of health services from high- to low-cost providers.

For much of the post-World War II era, the federal and state governments, together with many community leaders, sought to stimulate the construction and expansion of hospitals and ancillary facilities such as clinics and nursing homes to provide for the rapidly growing population that wanted and was able to pay for a higher level of health services. By the late 1960s, some observers had come to realize that, however measured, the earlier bed shortage was clearly a part of history. In many communities, many of the beds in use were in obsolete buildings and sooner or later would have to be replaced, but the further expansion of short-term hospital beds was no longer an issue. Indeed, a recent report by a committee of the Institute of Medicine concluded that the United States has too many hospital beds and that the early closure of 30,000 beds—about 3 percent of the total supply of short-term beds—could be effected without any risk of reducing needed services and would offer other considerable cost savings, approximating $1 billion annually.[44]

The first direct attack on controlling the expansion of facilities and services came with the 1972 amendments to the Social Security Act. The amendments provided that the federal government would henceforth reimburse hospitals for Medicare and Medicaid patients in new beds only if state authorities had issued a "certificate of need" authorizing the construction of these new beds. Many states also gave the regulatory authorities the right to disapprove any substantial capital improvement, even one involving only $100,000 of new investment. With this device, state regulatory authorities were able to slow the introduction or expansion of expensive new services such as open heart surgery, cobalt therapy, and the use of the CAT scanner for diagnostic work.

But in most jurisdictions these efforts constrained only hospital expansion, not the activities of private practitioners.

There is the anomaly, therefore, of a state agency's denying a hospital the right to purchase a costly CAT scanner at the same time that several physicians in the same area are installing them in their private offices.

The reformers justifiably insist that as long as hospitals are reimbursed for all their expenditures related to the provision of patient care—including liberal salaries and fringe benefits for their staffs, expanded programs for research and education, and community-directed services such as satellite clinics and genetic counseling—their costs will continue to spiral. The only prospect of containing this crucial component of total health expenditure is to find an alternative to full cost reimbursement.

In his *Letter* of January 1977, the president of the United Hospital Fund (New York), Dr. Joseph Terenzio, set forth the following alternative systems of reimbursement. The first is prospective budget review, in which the hospital negotiates in advance with the reimbursement agency and is able to keep any "savings" it is able to achieve. The second involves a uniform limitation on rate increases, an approach used by the federal government during the early 1970s, when the Economic Stabilization Program was in effect, and one that may be reinstated by the Carter Administration. A third variant is called "peer group ceilings." Hospitals are grouped according to the range and depth of services they provide—from major teaching institutions to a small 100-bed community hospital—and are paid at the average for their group. Another reimbursement classification reflects the number of admissions or the seriousness of the conditions of the patients.

Each of these alternatives seeks a balance between constraining the rate of increases in hospital expenditures and allowing for the considerable variability in the output of different hospitals both in the quantity and quality of the services they provide.

The most ambitious experimentation with hospital reimbursement has been the rate review efforts of Connecticut and Maryland. On the basis of several years' experience, these two states have concluded that their hospital costs have advanced less than the average. If we accept as a fact that the institution of a comprehensive system of rate review is likely to slow, at least for a time, the upward trend of hospital costs, how does such a control mechanism avoid the danger of impeding innovation, which usually requires higher outlays?

The third approach to cost containment, one accompanied by substantial clout, is to encourage a shift from high-cost to low-cost providers. The classic case involves a shift from treating patients in hospitals to treating them in nursing homes, in their own homes, or in physicians' offices. Over the years, modest gains have been achieved along these lines. Some physicians have increased the workup and the aftercare they provide in their own offices in an effort to reduce the number of days their patients must be hospitalized. Since home-care programs were first introduced, immediately after World War II, they have been expanded only marginally. While the last decade has seen a rapid expansion of nursing homes, most patients are direct admissions, not hospital transfers.

The usual explanation for the accelerated increases in costs has been the perverse effects of insurance, which reimburses patients when they are hospitalized and does not cover comparable services in other treatment settings. But that is clearly not the whole story: witness the reported difficulties that Great Britain has encountered in treating patients in the least costly environment. And for years the same has been true of the large municipal health care system in New York City, in which the expenses of the poor are covered entirely by public funds. Here, too, there are patients in high-cost short-term beds who could be treated just as well in a less costly facility, except that none are available.

The reimbursement mechanism has admittedly abetted the escalation of costs by encouraging patients to be treated in hospitals rather than in less costly settings. Nevertheless, we must also note the additional barriers intensifying these distortions, such as the absence of alternative facilities, the disinclination and inability of many families to provide long-term care for chronic patients at home, the conservatism of physicians who are loath to undertake many procedures outside of a hospital setting.

Each approach to cost containment—control over facilities, new reimbursement mechanisms, appropriate treatment settings—promises some relief, but in the opinion of the many economists none will prove effective. The economists believe that it will be necessary to reintroduce restraints on the consumer by forcing him to pay more of his expenses directly. The market-oriented economists are convinced that people will use more goods or services than they need if they do not have to pay for them out of their own pockets.

They believe that at the center of the cost escalation is the absence of constraint upon the patient or upon his physician which would discourage use of costly hospital care. Only a financial deterrent offers a real prospect for greater economy in hospital utilization. There are a variety of ways in which the consumer can be made to share the cost.

The more conventional approach involves such a deterrent as requiring the patient to pay half or all of the first day's cost of hospitalization, or requiring him to cover 20 percent of the total cost, as do many major medical insurance plans. Although some economists see merit in these approaches, others are less certain about their putative effectiveness, much less their desirability. Many health planners believe that people should be encouraged to seek health care without having to surmount a financial obstacle. Others question whether any reasonable approach to cost sharing could actually slow the rise of expenditures significantly.

During most of the post-World War II decades, the belief that there is no prospect for a significant improvement in the health care system without a substantially enlarged supply of physicians gained acceptance.

Since 1963, Congress has taken a series of steps to expand the output of health professionals, particularly physicians, in response to the national consensus that health care would lag as long as there was a shortage of physicians. Federal officials stated in the mid-1960s that the shortage of physicians was approximately 50,000. Through combined federal, state, and, to a lesser degree, voluntary efforts, the nation's medical education plant was substantially expanded; by the end of the 1970s, its annual physician output will be almost double that of a decade earlier.

When Congress finally passed the Health Professions Education Assistance Act in October 1976 (after several years of wrangling about the amount of service that individuals who received federal support during their training would have to contribute), the concern with the physician shortage had largely evaporated. The Act explains this by declaring, "There is no longer an insufficient number of physicians and surgeons in the United States and . . . there is no further need for affording preference to alien physicians and surgeons in admission to the United States." The last clause refers to FMGs, who in 1975 accounted for a high proportion of physicians in residency training as well as a high proportion of all newly licensed practitioners. In certain states such as Maine and New Jersey, they constituted up to 70 percent of newly licensed physicians.

Five years earlier, when Congress first provided direct support to schools training health professionals through the establishment of a system of capitation payments, it took an additional step. It decided to use the leverage of federal dollars to influence the type of training that medical graduates pursue. The federal government, convinced that the country needed more physicians who could provide primary care, decided to finance the establishment of residency programs in family practice.

The 1976 Act increases the involvement of Congress in problems of distribution with respect to both specialization and location. With respect to specialization, Congress directed the nation's medical schools to increase annually in their own and affiliated hospitals the proportion of first year residency positions in primary care (internal medicine, family practice, and pediatrics) so that by 1980, 50 percent of all residencies will be in primary care; otherwise, each school would thereafter be required to meet this goal. The power to enforce this directive is contained in the stipulation that federal capitation payments for students enrolled in the health professions schools, which will amount to some $250 million in 1980, will be contingent upon compliance with this redirection in residency training.

The second major thrust of the 1976 legislation is directed at encouraging young physicians to accept assignments for specified periods in shortage areas. These will be designated by the Secretary of HEW according to such criteria as the ratio of health professionals to population, infant mortality rates, access to health services, and the percentage of physicians employed by hospitals who are foreign medical graduates.

To achieve this objective, Congress has provided for increased authorization for the National Health Service Corps (NHSC) from $40 million to $200 million in a series of four annual increments. Students can receive stipends of $400 a month for living expenses (subject to upward adjustment) and have their tuition and other reasonable educational expenses paid. In return they are required upon graduation (with up to a three-year deferment for graduate studies) to serve in a shortage area for a minimum of two years. Each year of service will cancel one year of scholarship aid. There are stringent financial penalties placed on students who seek to buy themselves out of their contract.

The National Health Service Corps, established in 1970, has attempted to enroll as volunteers certain categories of health professionals with the aim of assigning them to "critical shortage areas." The principal incentives have been relatively high salaries—$32,000 a year for a young physician in addition to malpractice insurance and cancellation of loans incurred during his period of education—on the basis of one year of support for a year of service, subject to the enrollee's agreeing to serve a minimum period of two years.

Enrollees can choose between entering the Corps or accepting a position in a Public Health Service activity such as the Indian Service, the Coast Guard, or one of its own hospitals or clinics. Most volunteers choose the last category. In 1976 only 200 students who had been subsidized were serving in any location, and only 20 were in the National Health Service Corps. The 1976 Health Assistance Act tightened the terms of the contract, making it more difficult for enrollees to buy their way out, and in the face of higher tuition costs in medical school, the expectation is that the numbers available for placement in shortage areas will increase substantially.

The intent of Congress with respect to each of these programs aimed at improved manpower distribution is clear. It is using federal dollars to persuade hard-pressed medical schools and hard-pressed medical students to do what they have been unwilling to do up to now—to prepare for a career in primary care and to practice, if only for a time, in a shortage area.

Disappointed that its earlier large-scale efforts to expand the supply of physicians did not have the anticipated result of increasing the number of practitioners in shortage areas and of sufficiently shifting the balance in favor of primary care, Congress acted in 1976 to force the issue. We will defer till later consideration of the forces that will determine the success of this latest intervention by Congress to improve medical care through manipulation of manpower resources.

Medical reformers have contended for years that substantial gains in the effectiveness of health care delivery could be achieved by a series of structural, functional, and organizational changes:

—Greater emphasis upon ambulatory treatment as a substitute for inpatient care.
—Greater congruence between types of inpatient facilities and patients' medical needs, with an increase of nursing care facilities.
—The functional coordination of hospitals and other health care facilities into a regional system so that patients who require different levels of care may receive them at an appropriate facility.
—Increased participation of physicians in group practice, particularly prepaid groups.
—Reorganization of clinics and outpatient departments heavily frequented by the poor to permit greater continuity in patient-physician relations.

The growth of hospital insurance has skewed the delivery system in favor of inpatient treatment. While insurers, nonprofit and commercial, are experimenting with extending benefits to ambulatory services, particularly for diagnostic and posthospital care, progress has been slow because of the difficulty of differentiating between patients with routine illnesses and those requiring more complex diagnosis and care.

A related difficulty faces the federal authorites as they consider revising current regulations to permit individuals to enter a nursing home without a prior stay in a hospital. Clearly, the need for such admission could be determined in many instances without hospitalization, but the fear is that if the requirement of prior hospitalization were waived, many physicians would certify patients for nursing home care who could be cared for just as well in their own homes.

The goal of regionalization has been on the nation's agenda for health reform ever since the early 1930s, when the Commission on the Costs of Medical Care issued its bench mark report. But progress has been hampered by the need to develop on a voluntary basis linkages among different types of health institutions. Experience has shown that most institutions are amenable to enlarging their role, but few are willing to agree to a reduction in the scale and scope of their activities. While highly specialized health activities are usually concentrated in areas of high population density, there are few signs that new and vigorous efforts at greater regionalization will occur through voluntary agreements among institutions.

For many years, the American Medical Association and most state and county medical associations were unalterably opposed to prepaid group practice units and succeeded in inhibiting their growth. That opposition is now largely muted, although it has not been eliminated. In the last three years the number of enrollees in prepaid health plans has doubled from 4 to 8 million in response to encouragement from various sources, including the federal government, commercial insurance companies, medical schools, and physician and consumer groups.[45] With Kaiser-Permanente as the prototype and spurred by its favorable experience of providing comprehensive services at lower cost, based primarily on reduced use of hospitals, it is widely believed that solo practice will eventually yield to Health Maintenance Organizations (HMOs).

Some protagonists argue that the federal government must

act to amend the present legislation, which places the HMOs at a disadvantage with competing plans by requiring them to provide too broad a range of services. The proponents of HMOs further believe that more liberal subsidies are required to enable the HMOs to build up enrollments to a satisfactory level of 30,000 or more per unit. It is by no means certain that these changes would assure a marked growth of prepayment plans. The scattered evidence indicates recurrent difficulties with respect to enrollment, hospital relations, management problems, and quality control.

Medicaid, which enabled the poor to pay for care from physicians, clinics, or the outpatient departments and emergency rooms of hospitals, has often resulted in patients receiving inferior care at high cost to the government. The most egregious producers of poor services at high costs are the so-called Medicaid mills in ghetto areas which continue to thrive despite repeated public exposure. The organization of HMOs to serve the poor has been frequently recommended, but to date there has been little progress. The needs of the poor for health services far exceed the funds available for paying providers.

The current experimental program, financed by the Robert Wood Johnson Foundation in cooperation with various insurance companies that are providing loans for construction, will provide a test case of whether a significant potential exists for hospital-based ambulatory care that could contribute to better quality at lower cost. The presumption is that economies of scale are achievable, particularly in the diagnostic arena involving both personnel and equipment. But it may turn out that all types of care, including ambulatory care, in a hospital setting lead to cost escalations that are easier to control in solo or small group-practice situations.

Congress passed the National Health Planning and Resources Development Act of 1974 (PL 93-641) in December of that year. The aim of the legislation was to encourage the states and health service areas (HSAs) within the states to increase their roles in the planning process. It was expected that their greater involvement would lead to plans that would bring health resources and requirements into better balance and would lead to action programs that would improve the health care and health status of the population.

The legislation was particularly detailed. It laid down rules governing the membership of the planning bodies, providing a prominent place for consumers, and specifying the process for the designation of the HSAs. It established linkages among the levels of the planning hierarchy from the HSAs to the federal government, leaving open whether the individual HSA would be under public or voluntary leadership. Modest funding was made available to initiate the effort.

The system will probably not be operational until some time in 1978, but the limited number of competent planners, the excruciatingly small amount of local-area health data, tensions between city and suburb, rich and poor, white and nonwhite, established institutions and those in early stages of growth are early indicators that the new planning process is beset with difficulties. There are health issues on which an area-planning group should be able to reach a consensus. But the odds decline as the planning group seeks to act on issues of major concern to a powerful interest group, such as whether an established hospital should be permitted to relocate or expand. Experience does not generate optimism about the potentialities of a largely voluntary structure of planning. On the other hand, we must agree with Congress that the remodeling of the health care delivery system cannot be accomplished without the active participation of local groups.

This brings us to the fifth and last component of current

approaches to reform. A recent government publication states that "National Health Insurance (NHI) is probably the most crucial and compelling issue facing the American health care system today."[45] During the long and inconclusive battle over national health insurance that has been waged with varying intensity for over forty years, the vast expansion of nonprofit and commercial health insurance has revolutionized health care financing. The magnitude of the change is reflected in the fact that in 1975 consumers paid directly for less than one-third of all their personal health expenditures; the comparable figure for 1929 was 88 percent and for 1940, 82 percent. The present insurance system, then, may be described either as a pluralistic arrangement because of the coexistence of commercial, non-profit, and governmental (Medicare) programs, or as a make-shift structure that lacks universal coverage, comprehensive benefits, efficient administration, and budgetary controls.

In light of such differences in viewpoint, we should not be surprised to find a wide range of proposals directed to improving the situation.

The most modest proposal aims at the federal government's insuring against "catastrophic illness"; the most ambitious involves universal coverage in an NHI system that represents a major step toward comprehensive benefits. Other schemes fall between these extremes in coverage and benefits. A major point of difference arises with respect to the administration of NHI: at one extreme, the federal government would be the responsible agent; at the other, the states and private intermediaries would continue to have leading roles.

The proposals differ with respect to administration, financing, and payments to providers. The more radical favor federal direction of the system, financing through payroll taxes and the use of general revenues, and capitation payments to physicians who form prepayment plans. The more modest proposals favor a minimum disturbance in present arrangements: these prefer to rely on present insurance intermediaries, such as Blue Cross, to supplement existing financial arrangements by some form of federal-state contribution assisting the poor in obtaining coverage, and to modify the fee-for-service system for paying physicians and other providers.

In 1977 it seems unlikely that the more radical version of NHI, which would provide universal coverage, comprehensive benefits, federal administration, and tight budgetary controls, will soon be enacted. The condition of the federal budget and the mood of the taxpayer do not favor such an expanded commitment, even ignoring for the moment such additional questions as how such a far-reaching reform is likely to affect the efficiency and quality of the health delivery system. The more likely development is a restricted effort along the lines of insurance against catastrophic medical expenditures. Should Congressional action be delayed for several years, even this modest approach to NHI may become moot because of a further rapid expansion of "major medical" coverage. At present, this type of coverage is held by three-quarters of the nation's 180 million insured individuals, half of whom have insurance for over $100,000 of medical bills.[45]

What generalizations can be drawn from this capsule review of current efforts at health reform?

—A great deal of attention is being directed toward cost containment, but the results so far have been disappointing. However, serious and sustained efforts by third-party payors to exert a restraining influence on hospital expenditures are just beginning. It would be premature to conclude that these efforts will prove inconsequential.
—Congress, satisfied that the national pool of physician manpower is now adequate, has moved aggressively along three new axes: to restrict the inflow of foreign medical graduates; to force an expan-

sion in the number of primary care physicians; to develop a pool of medical school graduates for assignment to shortage areas through subsidization of undergraduate training. Time alone will tell whether the anticipated results of these efforts will lead to significant gains in the health care of the American people.

—A review of efforts to alter the health care delivery system has shown only modest progress in the expansion of prepayment plans and even less in the development of regional linkages among health facilities and in the improvement of ambulatory care.

—Two years ago the country implemented a new health-planning system based on state and local initiatives, but it will be several more years before an initial assessment can be made of the efficacy of the new program. Our review has suggested that voluntary agreements on a local level that affect the basic interests of key groups will not be easy to achieve.

—Finally, our review of the status of national health insurance leads us to question whether "its time has come." The review further highlights that NHI covers a wide range of alternative proposals, from a modest addition to the present structure to a truly revolutionary change in the American health care system.

At this point, it is no longer certain that significant health reform in the United States is achievable—if it ever was— through any single innovation, even through comprehensive national health insurance. The effective reform of the health care system will depend on the extent to which we can slow the rise in costs; determine what, if any, governmental intervention in the manpower market can contribute to improved care; experiment with new systems of health delivery; transform our planning mechanisms from paper exercises into active programs; and find ways of strengthening the health insurance system.

In sum, health reform stands revealed as a form of social intervention for which it is easier to specify goals than to design and implement effective methods for achieving them.

10

Restraints

THE LAST CHAPTER considered the principal thrusts of current health reform efforts in the United States. But no large and important social system—health, education, criminal justice, welfare, transportation—ever operates solely on its own. Each system is constrained by the values and understanding of the citizenry, the ease or difficulty of attracting financial resources, the attitudes and behavior of the professionals who provide the services, and the extent to which agreement or conflict characterizes the relations among key interest groups. These four determinants set the framework within which the goals of reform must be developed and implemented. The search for realism in health reform requires that each of these restraining forces be critically reviewed.

We will begin by asking: What is the relation between a significant improvement in the quantity and quality of health services available to the American people and the goals—longer life, continuing vitality, less pain, less discomfort, less anxiety—they seek to achieve through the health care system?

There are three possible answers. The first is that we do not know enough to develop credible answers. Science and medicine are open systems in which new knowledge is constantly being discovered and new techniques, based on the new knowledge, are constantly being developed. One cannot foresee the consequences of knowledge and techniques that have not yet been discovered. But the matter is not quite so intangible or elusive. Suppose we start with the dominant view about cellular growth and destruction, which holds that the range of human life cannot be extended. All members of a cohort will be dead around the hundredth year. But if the limits of human life could be extended to 125, 150, 200 years, a major structural change would have been achieved and all assumptions and deductions based on the 100-year optimum would become invalid. But as a distinguished scientist, Leonard Hayflick, recently argued, we can expect little or no change in the limits of human life.[46] The most that we can expect is continuing gains in the proportion of the cohort who approach the upper limit in reasonably good health. All efforts at health reform should, at least for the present and the indefinite future, be constrained by this reality.

A second view of the possible relation between the health care system and our health goals stresses the relative unimportance of therapeutic medicine for health compared with both positive and negative environmental determinants—such as real income, pollution, and individual behavior patterns, particularly those related to eating, exercise, work, sleep, alcohol. In recent years, British epidemiologists have emphasized the first set of factors, while Lester Breslow of the University of California in Los Angeles has stressed the second, pointing out that good health habits can add eleven years to longevity, which would raise the average life span of men from sixty-seven to seventy-eight.

Skeptics who question the advisability of investing ever larger sums in the health care industry call attention to a host of discouraging facts and figures: the net addition to longevity of less than two years that would result if cancer could be eliminated; the correlative fact that despite extensive efforts at research, early detection, and treatment, the death rate from cancer continues to rise from as yet unidentifiable causes; the relatively modest gains that are being registered in reducing the death rate for most diseases of the circulatory system. Since cancer and diseases of the circulatory system primarily afflict persons in the middle and upper age brackets, the years of productive life that can be added by scientific advances are proportionately fewer than would follow a comparable reduction in the deaths of young people from automobile accidents, suicide, and homicide. Skeptics also cite the fact that despite the vaunted progress of the health care industry, life expectancy of the adult male of thirty in the United States has increased only six years since the beginning of the century.[47] Clearly, the skeptics have a strong case.

A third viewpoint is at variance with the first two. Assume, it states, that the limits of human life are unlikely to be extended. Assume further that most of the gains that will be made in the future will consist of prolonging the lives of persons approaching the upper age limits. Assume also that the individual's life style is a major determinant of his health and longevity. Even if we accept these three premises, it is wrong to dismiss the substantial contribution that the health care system has been able to make to the life, vigor, and well-being of many citizens. It has permitted them to live longer and to function better than they would have without the benefits of modern medicine. We can challenge the proposition that because an event has occurred in the past, it will happen again. Nevertheless, there is good reason to anticipate further gains

from medical progress. Difficulties arise, however, in determining the level and path of national investment in health
research.

These opposing views can be summed up in two contrasting
propositions. The first is reflected in the observation of the
former chief economist of the American Medical Association,
Frank Dickinson, who pointed out that the principal gains of
modern medicine are to be read in the changing causes of
reported deaths. The second is the challenge posed by many
health reformers who ask what alternative expenditures by an
affluent public are likely to yield as much or more consumer
satisfaction than those which increase, even modestly, the
length and quality of a person's later years.

We now are face to face with the second important constraint which directly influences the shape of health reform—
and not only its shape, but also its direction and speed. What
is the financial situation, defined in terms of the consumer's
disposable income and the government's fiscal condition?

The heavy emphasis on "cost containment" suggests that
the American people may be reaching the end of their financial tether. Expenditures for health have increased from
around 4 percent of the GNP to over 8 percent in the last forty
years. Economists lean toward the view that we are rapidly
approaching the upper limits of expenditures on health, although two sophisticated analysts, Herbert Klarman and Uwe
Reinhardt, have challenged this conclusion and believe that
the health sector may grow until it accounts for 10 or even 12
percent of America's annual output.

But ours is a more limited concern. Whether the ceiling
turns out to be 9, 10, 11, or even 12 percent of the GNP, what
is the impact of an increasing financial stringency on health
reform? The growing concern with cost containment clearly
suggests that the flow of dollars into the health care industry is

more constricted than formerly, and that it is likely to become even more so in the future.

A second proposition is the inevitable large increase in federal health expenditures that looms ahead as a result of existing programs which must accommodate increasing numbers of persons eligible for Medicare and Medicaid and at the same time allow for future cost increases. *The Five Year Budget Projections* of December 1976, released by the Congressional Budget Office, anticipate an increase from $38.9 billion in Fiscal Year 1976 to $74.9 billion by Fiscal Year 1982.[48] In absolute terms, this is an increase of $36 billion without new programs; in percentage terms, it represents a rise of almost 100 percent in five years with no new program initiatives. The budget table from which the foregoing figures have been extracted provides an illuminating contrast: total federal expenditures are scheduled to rise by $173 billion, from $413 to about $586 billion or 41 percent, in the same period. Thus, at a minimum, expenditures for health are likely to increase at a rate one and a half times total federal expenditures.

Faced with these estimates, we can expect Congress to be cautious in responding to any proposal for health reform that requires an additional large increase in expenditures. The federal government will find it difficult to meet existing commitments and such new emergencies as are certain to arise.

A further financial constraint arises from the prospective difficulties of raising premiums for health insurance. At present, Blue Cross is a bigger supplier for General Motors than U.S. Steel. Both unions and employers are becoming keenly aware of the implications of costly health benefits, particularly because they increasingly preempt funds required for new benefits. The country may be still some distance away from the outer limits to which insurance premiums can be raised, but the total health bill that the employee now covers directly or indirectly cannot be ignored. Health costs represent a large bite into his real compensation.

An interesting aspect of group health insurance is that an increasing number of plans continue coverage for the first three months of a worker's unemployment, a period during which most persons who are laid off return to their jobs. In many families with a second worker, the family's coverage continues even if one wage earner remains unemployed for a longer period. Early in 1975 the National Commission for Manpower Policy inquired of HEW whether there was evidence of growing hardship for unemployed workers in obtaining medical care. The information furnished to the Commission indicated little more than marginal difficulties. There is no reliable study of what in fact did happen as a result of workers' losing their insurance because of unemployment. They may have postponed essential medical care. But one conclusion is incontestable: the severe recession did not usher in a crisis in hospital financing, although it put stress on many Medicaid plans that provide a backstop for workers in financial straits.

A related facet of the financing issue is the strong advocacy by certain labor leaders of a comprehensive plan for national health insurance on the ground that only such a plan will put a stop to the escalating health costs that are borne, if largely indirectly, by the American working man and woman.

As the discussion moves from speech-making to legislative drafting and the financial realities of what a comprehensive system of national health insurance would cost, the odds are strong that some union leaders will back off. Moreover, certain labor leaders are likely to oppose quietly any reforms that will reduce or eliminate their control over the management of health security funds, which they now exercise under collective bargaining arrangements.

These considerations concerning the interactions between money and health reform are suggestive rather than definitive. They point to a rising awareness in many sectors—government, business, labor—that the health care industry is currently consuming a significant and growing share of the dollars available for fringe benefits for workers and of the incremental expenditures of government. Both these perceptions, together with tautness in governmental budgets, suggest that the public's reaction to any significant health reform proposal and surely to one of the more ambitious versions will be conditioned by the price tag. A major reform would require an appropriation of additional dollars as well as a rechanneling of current dollars. Most estimates suggest that the new burden on the federal government's financial system would be about $100 billion for a comprehensive approach. Because of the necessity to make substantial realignments between present and potential contributors to the financing of health care, it may turn out to be easier to keep adding to the present mixed pattern of payments as required by the upward pressure of costs than to take on the more formidable task of restructuring and expanding the financial base of the entire system.

A critical objective of the proponents of major health reform is to establish greater equity in access to health services via a comprehensive system of national health insurance. This in turn would involve a substantial redistribution of health resources from the areas that are well endowed to those that are underserved. The experience of the last decade is significant. As a result of Medicare, Medicaid, and the extension and improvement of health insurance coverage, many low-income families succeeded in improving their access to the system. Their utilization of inpatient and outpatient services rose both absolutely and relative to higher income groups so that most of the preexistent gaps were eliminated.

However, we must not exaggerate the relation between larger expenditures, especially of public funds, and expanded services for low-income groups. Differences continue to exist between Medicaid expenditures per enrollee in the low-income Southern states and in the more affluent mid-Atlantic states. Significant differences are also found among federal-state beneficiaries, both with respect to admission to nursing homes and hospitals, and to the use of more expensive serivces such as surgery.

Two sets of forces account for the substantial per capita variation in health care utilization among regions. The first reflects cultural and societal forces that tend to keep utilization relatively low because of a conservative tradition among both the citizenry and the providers, especially with respect to hospital care. Living conditions also play a role. It is usually easier to care for an old person on a farm than in a crowded tenement.

The second set of forces reflects the distribution of health resources—hospital beds, physicians, clinics. Fewer resources lead to fewer services.

Gordon McLachlan, in his review of the experience of the United Kingdom under the National Health Service, makes the telling point that the regional imbalance of health, resources that marked the beginning of the period still exists more than a quarter of a century later.[49]

Formidable problems would attend any effort to narrow the differentials in the distribution of health resources in the United States—a first condition for major progress toward equalization in the delivery of health services. When it appeared that the Kennedy-sponsored health manpower bill, with its stringent provisions for physician allocation, was likely to be passed, the powerful California Congressional delegation met in special session to assess its potential effects upon their state. Their purpose was to agree on tactics to amend or derail the bill in order to eliminate its deleterious effects on their constituents. In the face of such political realities, it is visionary to expect an early or substantial redistribution of the nation's health resources from the more to the less affluent states.

Even if a significant regional redistribution of health resources could be achieved, equal access and use of health services would still be illusory. Differences in family income, governmental entitlements, and other factors would still result in unequal access.

Shortly after World War II, Topeka, Kansas, had three psychiatric facilities. One was the Menninger Clinic, which provided inpatient care including individual psychotherapy at a cost of about $25,000 per annum. Another was a Veterans Administration hospital, in which per patient cost averaged $2,200 annually. The third was a state institution that operated at a cost of under $600 per patient per annum. Here is a variation of expenditures per patient of 1 to 40. One need not claim that these large dollar differences of outlay were directly translated into differences in quality of health services rendered, but no adjustment can obscure the advantages of the wealthy over the poor.

An affluent democracy has every reason to strive to narrow existing differentials among groups and regions in access to care and in the quality of services. But our nation would be well advised to avoid promising a basic egalitarianism in health care. It cannot achieve this goal without altering its basic values and institutions, including the right of people to use their money as they see fit and to pursue their careers wherever they choose. One might argue that, even if a democracy succeeded in becoming egalitarian, those in positions of political power would still have preferred access to health care.

One final observation on equity: one must weigh the costs of reducing inequities in health services against the diversion of resources that could be used to accomplish other important goals. When the poor are asked on opinion surveys to identify their major needs, they almost never single out improved health care. This may reflect their inability to understand that their underemployment and low income are linked to the poor state of their health. Nevertheless, they may be right in their perception that they stand to gain more from greater societal efforts directed to employment, income maintenance, housing, or public security than from increased expenditures for health services. I would argue (although I have no proof) that the rapid expansion of the Food Stamp Program since 1970 has contributed more to improving the health of the poor than new or improved health care programs.

So far we have considered briefly the constraints to health reform arising from the public's lack of understanding of how the system operates and the increasing stringency in financial resources. We will now assess a third constraint: the society's ability to use incentives and controls to change the role of the physician, who dominates the decision-making process.

In the preceding chapter, we discussed the recent legislation directed to obtaining one year of service from a young physician for each year of subsidized medical training. Because the program is new, and because most of the "indentured" group is still in the pipeline, it is too early to judge this effort. But several points are worth noting. All earlier efforts by the federal government, state governments, and foundations to trade support for service have had at best limited success. In one way or another, physicians have succeeded in avoiding service in unattractive locations. However, the record is not altogether bleak. The Armed Services have had good results in enforcing their contracts with health professionals, perhaps because they enrolled them at the beginning of their training in the reserves.

The National Health Service Corps faces difficulties that go beyond holding physicians to their obligations. These difficulties relate to selecting areas or institutions that are short of health personnel. The shift in terminology from "critical shortage" to "medically underserved" is suggestive. So far, over 1,650 areas have been designated and 700 have been approved as assignment sites. Since many underserved locations and institutions may lie cheek to jowl with affluent areas—a ghetto bordering on a high-income neighborhood— it takes little imagination to envision that assignees will serve more than the needy.

The most general statement that can be made at this early stage of the program is that government does best when it moves with the market. Here, as elsewhere, efforts at health reform should be moderated by judgments about the ability of government to affect the behavior of physicians when it moves against the market.

The determining role of physicians in the operation of all health care systems can be readily demonstrated. During World War II, for example, the Chief of Staff of the Army had five stars while the Surgeon General had two. Nevertheless, the Medical Department enjoyed a high degree of autonomy. A cynical explanation would highlight that medical corps officers determined whether other officers, including those in the highest rank, were physically fit to continue on active duty and, if not, whether they should be retired with a disability compensation that in the past was worth many tens of thousands of dollars. The alternative explanation would be that even in a hierarchical military environment, the top leadership realizes that it cannot effectively control the work of professionals, and professionals are therefore permitted wide latitude to manage their own activities.

The importance of the hospital in the U.S. health care system and the physician's role in its evolution and expansion should be noted. As Professor Mark Pauly of Northwestern University has suggested, the hospital offers the physician a work environment that permits him to optimize his income by economizing in the use of his time.[50] It also offers him a large support system free of charge, which includes expensive technical equipment as well as interns and residents who relieve him of much routine work with his patients. Prior to the introduction of Medicare and Medicaid, there was a traditional *quid pro quo* between the community-supported hospital and the staff physician. The physician, especially the urban physician, served for many years in the outpatient department of the hospital, treating the poor free of charge, in order to qualify for a staff appointment that carried privileges of referring private patients for admission and treatment. Subsequently, as a member of the staff, he was also responsible for the care of ward patients. All of this free service became monetarized by Medicare and Medicaid, one more example of the unanticipated consequences of large-scale reforms without adequate planning and experimentation.

Independent studies of both the Canadian and the American health care systems have estimated that the addition of a single physician into the system generates new expenditures of around $250,000 annually. This helps to explain why the Canadian government, in an effort to stem its rapidly rising health expenditures, has reduced to a trickle the inflow of foreign physicians. The Health Professions Educational Assistance Act of 1976, however, with its provisions for reducing the immigration of foreign medical graduates into the United States, stemmed less directly from the desire to slow further cost generation than to assure residency slots for American physicians.

Various efforts at cost containment have been directed to

slowing the rise of physicians' fees and income by changing existing methods of payment, by the review of patient records to determine whether treatments provided were medically indicated, and by tightening procedures to detect and eliminate fraud. Although various efforts have been made by the federal and state governments and nongovernmental third-party reimbursing organizations to recalculate the basis for paying physicians with an aim of reducing their average fee, these attempts have at best retarded only slightly the substantial and sustained increase in physicians' incomes. Average fee, however, is only one determinant of physicians' income. The other important variable under a fee-for-service system is the number and types of treatment rendered. Since responsibility for patient care rests with the physician, he is in a position to justify any reasonable treatment plan. The most third-party reimbursers can hope to accomplish is to catch up with those who engage in outright fraud or whose patterns are at marked variance with those of their peers. However, these efforts, even if they were more successful than at present, would do relatively little to moderate the trend of physicians' earnings.

It does not follow, however, that a system of prepayment based on capitation or the employment of physicians at a fixed salary will solve the problem of excessive earnings. The Health Insurance Plan (HIP), New York City's long-established prepayment plan, has necessarily been staffed with part-time physicians who devote the minimum agreed upon time to enrollees because of their concern with expanding their private practices, which they carry on alongside their HIP duties. Kaiser-Permanente has successfully prevented staff members from pursuing private practice, but at a cost. On the one hand, Kaiser-Permanente has had difficulty in attracting and retaining certain scarce specialists who have little or no incentive to join a salaried group unable to offer them career opportunities equal to those they can enjoy on the open market. For those who do join and stay, Kaiser-Permanente has been forced to trade time for money. The work week, when adjusted on an annual basis for paid vacations and time off to attend professional meetings and other educational activities, is considerably shorter than the average for physicians in private fee-for-service practices.

Although the individual physician does not usually calculate what he believes he is entitled to earn and shape his practice accordingly, under the favorable supply-demand circumstances that have prevailed since World War II the profession as a whole has had little difficulty in meeting its expanding income goals. The changed demand and supply relations with respect to physicians' services that may develop in the future could alter this situation. However, recent moves by specialty societies to control the inflow of foreign medical graduates underscore the leaderships' desire to protect the high earnings of their members.

Since physicians have considerable scope to determine the demand for their services and therefore the size of their incomes, it is sound social policy to maintain a level physician supply and to tolerate their high earnings, which will have the ancillary advantage of discouraging overdoctoring. The alternative response, generally espoused by economists, is to increase the supply in the belief that it will lead to lower fees. However, as we have seen, it is not clear that lower fees will result in lower earnings. Even if they did and even if the average physician earned somewhat less than previously, an enlarged supply of physicians would add substantially to the total costs of the system.

In the context of health reform, we should consider whether economic incentives are likely to influence the choice either of specialty or location of practice. At present, we need to know more about the economic and noneconomic forces that determine the selection of specialty training. Certainly, potential earnings play a role, but their importance is hard to measure in relation to the host of personal and institutional factors that impinge on specialty selection.

It is easier to assess the role of potential earnings in physicians' choices of locations. During the past several decades, when most physicians had little difficulty in earning good incomes wherever they settled, the earnings factor had only modest importance. This does not imply that reimbursing agents in California should not adjust their fee schedules in favor of physicians who are willing to locate in the inland areas, since the vast majority prefer to live close to the Pacific Ocean. Nevertheless, we should not expect that even a radical change in fee schedules would, under present circumstances, significantly alter the distributional pattern.

The market always influences behavior, even among professionals—such as physicians who are in a protected relationship and can exert considerable influence over the demand for and the price of their services. Hence those concerned with health reform must appreciate the limits of using market mechanisms to alter the behavior of physicians.

We have called attention to the pervasive influence of physicians on the way hospitals operate, since it is they who largely determine the range and quality of the services provided and play a major if indirect role in affecting the decisions of the administrator and the trustees.

Organized into county and state medical societies, physicians are a powerful force in shaping legislation and in formulating the rules and regulations governing not only their own conduct but also that of all other professional groups involved in the delivery of health care. For instance, a state medical society must be neutralized before significant changes can be introduced in the range of activities that registered nurses are permitted to perform.

In the past, the American Medical Association, operating at the national level, was regarded by informed observers of the Washington scene as having more influence on Congress and the administration than any other lobby. Recently, internal fissures have strained the hegemony of organized medicine. The academic and research components, organized into the Association of American Medical Colleges, have pursued their priority objectives with only loose coordination with the AMA. Many physicians, especially among the growing ranks of those who are institutionally based, no longer belong to the AMA.

Weakened as it is by splits in its own ranks, by successive defeats in the political arena, by the defensive positions that have been forced upon it by regulatory agencies, by a reduced treasury, and by lessened public esteem, organized medicine nevertheless retains considerable clout. It still is able to beat back most attempts that aim to alter the long-standing relations between physician and patient, to restrict the rights of the profession to practice according to its own goals, or to weaken its economic position. On each of these three major points, organized medicine remains strong.

The question that follows logically is: what scope does a democratic society have to alter its health care system in the face of a well-organized professional group strategically positioned to influence the decision-making process at every level of society?

In countries with a nationalized system of health care, such as Great Britain, there is only one effective source of payment for health services. The distribution of the resources made available by Parliament among competing claimants, from consultants to ward attendants, however, remains a matter of contention by competing interest groups, among whom the medical profession occupies a strong position. As we move away from the broad allocation of funds to more technical considerations, such as the number and types of professionals to be trained, the choice of program alternatives as between therapeutic medicine and public health, the direction of research, and numerous other decisions, we find that in all these matters the leaders of the medical profession have a dominant voice.

Every profession is well positioned to determine its own future. Planning for health reforms must reckon with this basic fact: physicians alone are able to control the professional work of physicians.

This brings us to the fourth major constraint on health reform. Although organized medicine has a unique influence on the restructuring of the health care system by its power to veto or modify many reforms, a major proposal such as national health insurance involves other powerful interest groups—including commercial and nonprofit insurance carriers, the hospital establishment, particularly community hospitals, and the pharmaceutical industry—as parties of the first part. In addition, planning for major reforms must also take into account the attitudes and interests of the business community, organized labor, consumer organizations—specifically those concerned with health—and various health specialists inside and outside of government whose contributions are needed to flesh out specific reform proposals.

In addition to the foregoing, each of which contains a range of conflicting interests, many other groups will insist that the legislators hear their views in the event that the prospective reforms threaten adverse effects on their work or income. These range from religious groups that operate health facilities to professional organizations such as the American Nurses Association. If follows, therefore, that any large-scale reform requires the building of a national consensus.

In assessing the prospects of such a large-scale reform as national health insurance, it would be necessary to estimate the probability of gaining consensus among the principal groups with major stakes in the health care system—providers, payors, consumers. If we look back at the developments of the U.S. health care system since the end of World War II, we see that major pressure on the federal government to act was limited to the single case of Medicare. There was no ready alternative whereby older people could meet their large health expenditures. The other interventions by the federal government had less political urgency. Unless we can design an approach that will provide an incentive for the major interest groups to trade present power for future influence, there is little prospect that any large-scale proposal for reform can gain the political support required for enactment.

The passage of new legislation is a necessary but not sufficient condition to alter the health care delivery system of the United States. Congress can legislate new structures and agencies into existence; it can entitle new groups of citizens to a range of services; it can appropriate funds to help achieve these objectives. But specific health services can be delivered only by local providers to local citizens, and this represents the most critical constraint on all reforms.

We have suggested earlier that improvements in the delivery of health services at the local level involve many complex adjustments, including changes in the behavior of providers and consumers, the shift of health resources, new linkages among regional institutions, the establishment of new modes of service delivery, changes in incentives and constraints.

Consciousness-raising, understanding, and reforms are interdependent and interacting. This chapter has sought to illuminate four critical constraints on reform: the equivocal relation between the expansion of health care services and the improvement of the nation's health; the implications of "tight money" for the underwriting of expensive new reforms; the critical role of the medical profession in the operation of the health care system, not least in efforts to reform it; the numerous and heterogeneous interest groups with major stakes in the system that will thwart a consensus for reform unless public dissatisfaction reaches high intensity.

Although such a consensus does not now exist, less heroic efforts to improve the current system should be initiated. This is the concern of the next chapter.

11

Recommendations

SINCE unresolved tensions exist between the forces favoring major health reforms and the restraints that stand in their way, the odds favor the process of continuing marginal reforms rather than revolutionary changes. This chapter will set forth a limited number of objectives that such marginal reforms might address and changes that are needed that would require modest additional resources, and that promise worthwhile results.

At present, there are three major proposals for health reform on the nation's agenda, each of which commands considerable support because each is seen as an important building block to broadening access to health services without placing a severe financial burden on the users or the funders. The three proposals are, respectively, catastrophic health insurance; long-term care for the elderly and the disabled; and comprehensive health insurance benefits for mothers and children (Kiddicare).

A few words about each will help point up the challenges that the nation faces in seeking solutions for improved coverage for these groups. A recent analysis by the Congressional Budget Office (January 1977) facilitates the appraisal of catastrophic health insurance.[51] It reveals that a significant number of persons incur large expenditures for health services, measured either in terms of costs of over $5,000 or 15 percent or more of their income. The analysis estimates that about 7 million persons will have out-of-pocket expenses of more than 15 percent of their income for health care in the coming year. The principal cause of these large expenses is the fact that about 1.3 million persons will be in nursing homes for longer than six months and that over half of the total cost of this care, approximating $15 billion, will be paid for directly by them or their families.

A plan to cover the costs of care after 150 days of hospitalization with outlays in excess of $2,000 per person would cost between $13 and $14 billion. This plan would still leave substantially uncovered the 26 million persons without hospital insurance and the 19 million families whose income is below the median and whose sole protection is hospital insurance. A variation of the foregoing, which would cost slightly more, would protect low-income families against expenditures exceeding 15 percent of their incomes, but would rely on middle-income families to protect themselves through private coverage.

For approximately double the cost, or for an estimated $33 billion, it would be possible for private insurance to provide adequate coverage for low-income families and better coverage for catastrophic illness in middle-income families.

A program to provide comprehensive coverage for all income groups whose expenditures for health care exceed 5 percent of family income, however, would involve an estimated cost of $130 billion, and even then the catastrophic costs of long-term illness would still not be covered.

These alternatives point up a few simple facts: any attempt

to protect all of the public against excessive medical expenditures is difficult to design and would be exceedingly costly to implement. The higher the dollar outlays or percentage of family income to be covered by the individual or his family, the lower the cost of catastrophic insurance to the community. Close to half the population has substantial major medical insurance, which provides protection against high medical expenditures. But none of the plans described above, not even the most expensive, provides coverage for long-term care, which is a major reason why families face catastrophic expenses.

The long-term care issue has also been analyzed by the Congressional Budget Office (February 1977).[52] The boundaries are difficult to define since they must include both health and social services required by the elderly and disabled, services that can be provided in a nursing home, in their own homes, or in an intermediary facility such as a sheltered living arrangement. Because of the wide spectrum of services that the elderly and the disabled may require, from constant care for the bedridden to an occasional visit by a social worker for the ambulatory, there is no reliable basis for estimating the universe of need or the level of need. Total expenditures by all levels of government for long-term care in 1975 totaled around $6 billion, and private expenditures were somewhat higher, around $7 billion. A combination of factors—the increasing number of older persons, greater utilization of services, and continuing inflationary pressures—will probably lead to a doubling of these expenditures by 1980.

The Congressional Budget Office explored three options. The most modest contemplates liberalizing home care benefits under Medicare and mandating a minimum of home care services under Medicaid. The initial costs would be several billion dollars by the early 1980s and would increase thereafter.

An approach providing increased coverage for long-term care for all aged and disabled (the highest risk groups) would result in large expenditures if those entitled to receive benefits under the legislation were to utilize them heavily. By 1980, the cost could be in the $12 billion range and might go as high as $40 billion or possibly $50 billion by 1985.

A third option advanced by the Congressional Budget Office aims to limit the rise of expenditures through appropriations. The federal government would combine hospital and nursing home expenditures for long-term care and social services, under Title XX of the Social Security Act, into a federal-state program aimed at encouraging the states to experiment with different ways of providing services. The additional federal cost under this approach might be kept within a $5 to $10 billion range by 1985.

Several points stand out: the number of older and disabled persons who need long-term care will inevitably grow. Currently, individuals and their families carry the major responsibility of paying for this care. An approach aimed at broadening entitlements to long-term care for these groups would prove expensive. On the other hand, unless the present system is modified and strengthened, increasing numbers will not receive the care they need.

The third proposal that is attracting considerable attention is the National Health Insurance for Mothers and Children Act (95th Congress, S.370), known as the Kiddicare bill, which was reintroduced in the Senate and the House early in 1977 by Senator Javits and Representative Scheuer. Parenthetically, it should be noted that this proposal has long been a favorite with those who believe that the path to national health insurance requires staging and that the goal cannot be achieved in one giant step forward. The first major step was Medicare; the second was Medicaid; the third should be coverage for mothers and children. At that point, the protagonists hope and expect that the public will recognize the importance of taking whatever further actions are required to bring the remaining sectors of health care coverage within a single comprehensive insurance system.

The 1977 bill has several features aimed at the immediate goal of both assuring better health service to mothers and children and of serving as a building block for a comprehensive system. It is universal in its entitlements; the benefits are comprehensive; the financing is via payroll taxes. To enhance its prospects of passage, however, the sponsors plan to use private insurance carriers who will make direct payments to providers on the basis of approved fee schedules. Prospective rate setting is encouraged, but experimentation with capitation is mandatory for hospitals. A 10 percent copayment by the patient is required, except for preventive services to children, where capitation is used, and for the poor.

The major thrust of the bill is to cover the costs of all the health needs of children up to the age of eighteen and of all women during pregnancy and for twelve weeks thereafter. For children, every type of service is covered—preventive, diagnostic, therapeutic, and rehabilitative—in every type of setting—home care, nursing home, hospital. The full range of services includes laboratory work, drugs, appliances, mental health, social services. The chief exceptions are othodontia and dental services for children under four. As a quality-control measure, the bill stipulates that no payment will be made for major surgery unless it is performed by a board-eligible or board-certified surgeon. There are some limitations on the duration of benefits with respect to home care, nursing home care, and the utilization of rehabilitative and psychiatric services.

The cost of the program, estimated by the staff of Senator

Javits, its sponsor, is between $9 billion and $11 billion, which would be covered by a tax of .1 percent on wages paid by both employer and employee, and .1 percent of the income of the self-employed. There is to be no upper limit on either wages or income.

The proponents of the bill offer the following rationale. Many children and pregnant women are not now receiving essential services because they do not have the means to pay for them. This particularly hurts those whose income barely exceeds the eligibility limit for Medicaid. In terms of both outcome for the individual and costs to the society, it is better to take preventive and corrective action as early as possible. This bill would help to correct the distortions of spending so many of the health dollars on elderly persons. The bill also avoids the difficulties engendered by a means test, such as that used under Medicaid, by making entitlements universal and comprehensive.

Three major recommendations, then, for the reform of the health care system are in the planning stage or in the legislative hopper: catastrophic insurance, long-term care, maternal and child care. We will consider each within the earlier developed matrix of access, quality, cost, and equity.

With respect to access, underwriting long-term care for the elderly and the disabled would result in a large expansion in outlays and facilities, since much of the present costs for such care are now paid for by the individual or his family with many patients being cared for at home. Liberal public financing would probably encourage a rapid expansion of nursing home facilities to provide the required additional capacity.

The effect upon access is less clear with respect to Kiddicare. Unquestionably there would be some, possibly a considerable, increase in utilization of services, especially by children who require costly rehabilitative, mental, and dental services. But whether additional specialized facilities and services can be developed quickly is not clear; nor is it clear whether and to what extent the parents of children who need long-term continuing services will utilize them. The record of the Crippled Children's program and Community Mental Health Clinics points to the need for caution with respect to persons making full use of available services.

Catastrophic insurance is not directly aimed at increasing access but seeks to ease the financial burden of those who have undergone costly treatment. Nevertheless, the availability of insurance would unquestionably increase the utilization of expensive services, which currently are not provided to a wide range of patients.

The maternal and child care bill aims at quality assurance not only by attempting to provide care for children when their conditions can be most effectively treated, but also by the safeguards governing decisions involving surgery that are written into the law. By following the route of fee-for-service and free choice of provider, this bill would continue in the path of Medicaid rather than follow the early Crippled Children's program, which aimed at closer control over the providers of specialized services.

There is little basis for believing that the preconditions, in terms of experience, data, standards, and control mechanisms, are established for a rapid expansion of long-term care services that would result in a significant gain in quality. Such an expansion might even lead to a proliferation of marginal and substandard facilities.

Catastrophic insurance does not directly intersect with the quality issue. We could postulate, however, that if additional dollars were linked to an effort at quality control, a contribution to that end might be made.

The probable impact of the passage of one or another of

these proposals on cost containment is the easiest to assess. Each involves a marked increase in total program expenditures as well as in the federal share, and each is likely to speed cost escalation. Since these several proposals could be passed in a more or less expensive version, there is no way of calculating ahead of time their gross and net costs, but the estimates developed suggest additional annual expenditures of at least $10 billion for maternal and child care and $30 billion each for an intermediate type of catastrophic insurance and long-term care (which overlap in part). Since the total annual federal contribution to health care is currently in the low $40 billion range, the passage of a major catastrophic or long-term care bill could quickly lead to a doubling of that expenditure.

The direct costs to the nation and the federal government would be the beginning, not the end, of the cost impact. The experience with Medicare and Medicaid indicates that the institution of such large new expenditures will lead to a substantial escalation of the total cost structure.

Finally, a word about equity. Each of the proposals would make some contribution to improving the range and possibly the quality of services available to low-income consumers. Gains in equity would depend initially on how the catastrophic proposal is written—it could single out either low-income or middle-income families for relief. Both the expansion of long-term care and maternal and child care services would probably result in a shift toward more health care services for low-income persons, particularly if the unorthodox financing plan proposed in the Kiddicare bill were to survive Congressional action. Nevertheless, the gains in equity should not be exaggerated. The very poor find it difficult to obtain access to quality health care even when the government has entitled them to a range of services; those who earn enough to pay taxes will have to contribute the additional sums required to cover the sizable expenditures that the new measures will engender. If the current regressive Social Security tax system is used to finance these expansions, the gains in equity may be modest indeed except for the lowest wage earners.

Congress might be well advised to move with caution. The increased expenditures and general cost escalation are certain consequences; greater access, quality, and equity are problematic.

Nevertheless, a positive approach can be developed. If the continued expansion of major medical insurance were relied upon to provide reasonable protection for the middle class, Congress could seek remedies for those with inadequate or no hospital insurance. With respect to long-term care, the modest proposal of the Congressional Budget Office, which recommends a federal-state grant-in-aid program to encourage local experimentation with improved ways of providing comprehensive services for older and disabled persons, appears sensible. We must learn how to provide essential services in a less costly fashion so that we do not continue to encourage institutionalization, the least desirable approach for most recipients.

With respect to maternal and child care services, before a new quasi-independent health insurance system for children and pregnant women is established, improved entitlements under Medicaid should be explored.

The proposals we have reviewed—catastrophic insurance, long-term care, and maternal and child care—have much in common with the major health reforms of the mid-1960s that led to the passage of Medicare and Medicaid. They involve the expansion of entitlements for specified groups; large-scale financial outlays by the federal government; an effort toward greater equity by improving the access, quality, and financing of health care for low-income groups.

The common threads in the three proposals are the leadership role of the federal government in initiating and implementing health reforms; the anticipated gains from new financing mechanisms; the targeted goals that each measure addresses. All three proposals ignore in whole or in part the specific institutional and personnel changes that would have to be effected in every community in the United States where people receive health care services. New and improved services may depend on legislation in Washington and in state capitals, but the last decades of reform efforts clearly indicate that legislation can only modify the existing delivery system. It cannot, by itself, create a new delivery system and surely not one that follows the legislative intent.

Since legislation alone can alter the delivery system only marginally, we will next consider what other steps might be taken to improve health care delivery to underserved groups. Clearly, such an approach must be highly selective, but once we have identified the specific paths for reform, the reader will have an alternative to the heroic health care interventions that have characterized the last decades and continue to dominate the national stage.

The health needs of the following four groups will be reviewed to assess the prospects of reforms that might be both desirable and feasible: the rural poor, the urban poor, children in low-income families, the aged. The four groups overlap to some degree, but we will focus on the unique characteristics of each group.

In each case, we will consider how the new services can be provided, how they can be paid for, and how their quality can be assured. No reform that speaks to one or two of these dimensions is adequate; all three goals must be considered together.

There is consensus among both the experts and the public that the rural poor represent an underserved population. The thrust of the Health Professions Educational Assistance Act of 1976 is to bring physicians to rural areas. It may be that federal intervention will succeed, although earlier efforts by foundations, state governments, and the substantial Sears Roebuck program to bring practitioners to the rural areas had negligible success.

During the past four years, I twice visited Alabama at the request of the Regional Medical Program to assess the alternatives for improving health care for the medically indigent. I was dismayed to find that the state's plan provided not only for the early opening of a second medical school in Mobile (it is now in operation) but also for two additional medical schools. In my view, this is the wrong strategy. The production of a large number of physicians in a state is no guarantee that they will practice there if more attractive alternatives exist or, if they stay, that they will provide services for the poor. I believe there is a mutual antipathy between physicians and the poor that can be overcome only in settings where physicians do not earn their living through fees for service.

I advised the Regional Medical Program in Alabama that if the effort to improve health care for the rural population were shifted from the expansion of medical schools to improving the state's public health nurse corps, everybody would benefit—the taxpayer, the rural poor, the provider community. This would involve a multifaceted program: expanding the number of nurses, raising their salaries, providing nurse-practitioner training, furnishing these new practitioners with state cars, and assigning them to rural areas without physicians to deliver first-level care. Under such a plan, when a nurse encounters an indigent patient requiring care beyond her skill, she would be authorized to arrange for appropriate transportation to the nearest health facility.

Some critics will argue that such a system condemns the

poor to an inferior quality of care because they do not have ready access to a physician. Two points can be made in rebuttal. It must be demonstrated, first, that physicians can be enticed to practice among the rural poor, which I do not believe is feasible; and, second, that the nurse-practitioner provides a lower quality of care, again a presumption that is not self-evident.

There are many possible variations to the system outlined above. Nurse-practitioners might be teamed up with individual physicians in the area. Or they might be linked to a network of physicians whom they would be able to consult whenever they needed support. But the principle is that improved health services for the rural poor need not be sought only through the forced assignment of physicians to practice among people and in an environment they prefer to avoid. There are alternatives potentially less costly and more effective.

The problems of the urban poor are different. Those who need health services usually live within a short distance of large concentrations of health resources, including large numbers of practitioners. But the practitioners who continue an urban-based practice cater primarily to affluent and middle-class patients, not to the poor. The ratio of practitioners to ghetto patients is as low as, or frequently lower than, the physician-patient ratio in sparsely settled rural areas.

The urban poor have only two options. They can obtain ambulatory care from groups of physicians who have moved into their neighborhood with the intent of closing the gap created by the disappearance of private practitioners. These groups, often justifiably called "mills" because they seek to maximize their revenues by treating the largest number of patients, render care that is at best mediocre and at worst dangerous. The extent to which the treatment of the poor is concentrated among a small proportion of physicians is suggested by the Medicaid experience in New York City, which revealed that less than 4 percent of the city's active physicians accounted for approximately two-thirds of all billings for Medicaid patients.[53]

The principal alternative setting in which the urban poor, especially in large metropolitan centers, obtain ambulatory care are the outpatient departments and emergency rooms of voluntary and public hospitals. As noted earlier, such care often has serious drawbacks: the inability of the patient to see the same physician on return visits; the lack of coordination among physicians who treat a patient with multiple conditions; the long waiting time; the inability of the physician to retrieve relevant patient records so that procedures are often duplicated or therapeutic interventions are inadequate.

A beginning has been made to broaden the options of the urban poor through the development of community health clinics, which at least in theory can make effective use of nurse-practitioners and health auxiliaries as partial replacements for hard-to-attract-and-retain physicians. But most of the experiments have encountered difficulties as a result of leadership squabbles, uncertain funding, resistance of the clientele to physician extenders, and lack of suitable hospital backup. Despite these difficulties, it should prove possible, under either municipal or local community leadership, to provide primary care at costs far below the $50 reimbursement cost that teaching hospitals now demand for a clinic or emergency room visit. The major barriers to reform are political will and skill. Those who benefit from the present dollar flows do not want to see them rechanneled, and often the political leverage and organizational know-how needed to rechannel them are lacking. The required solutions must be developed locally. They cannot be legislated at state capitals or in Washington.

Members of the third underserved group are the children of the poor, both rural and urban. Public health officials have recently become concerned about the relatively low rates of immunization and other evidences of lack of essential health care services for these children. The experiences under Head Start revealed the advantages of using the preschool setting to diagnose and refer urgent health problems that were being neglected. The United States has never had an effective school health program. A good start for reforms aimed at improved health care for children of low-income families would be to strengthen the school health systems or to scrap them and start anew.

The maternal and child health bill provides for dental services other than orthodontia for children above the age of four. As we have seen, the largest remaining discrepancy in the utilization of health care between high- and low-income groups involves dental services. If the American people are serious about reducing this gap, a sensible way to make a large-scale effort would be to increase dental services for the children of low-income families. We could begin by encouraging the states and localities to experiment with one of three patterns: dental services provided in the school, in near-by clinics, or in private offices.

The programs should be structured to encourage the use of dental auxiliaries for first-level care, and payment arrangements should aim at some form of capitation. There should be an arrangement in most areas for dentists in private practice to assume responsibility for some of the large additional workload. We could anticipate lessened opposition to carefully designed plans in which private practitioners participate and have supervisory responsibilities.

The federal government, in association with selected states, might consider a series of experimental programs aimed at exploring the strengths and weaknesses of alternative modes of dental service delivery, financing arrangements, and quality control. The nation should not venture into this unknown area of subsidized dental care delivery without some prior experimentation.

There are, of course, many other shortcomings in the health care of children from low-income homes, ranging from the early diagnosis and treatment of hearing defects to the prevention of adolescent pregnancies. Many of these shortcomings could be moderated by enforcing present federal regulations requiring the screening of children in families on Medicaid and by expanding services covered by Medicaid.

The fourth group singled out for special attention are older persons who use a disproportionate amount of the total services the health system provides. A rough estimate is that people over sixty-five use about one and a half times more services than the rest of the adult population. Although the higher prevalence of chronic illness among older persons explains part of this differential, other factors also play a role: the free time at their disposal, which leads to their visiting a physician to relieve loneliness and to gain reassurance, and the availability of Medicare, which covers much of the cost. Reference was made earlier to the fact that about one half of all ambulatory visits are for trivial conditions. To this finding we should add the fact that about one quarter of all Medicare dollars for hospital care is expended on patients who die within twelve months after their hospitalization.

Our concern here is less with the wasteful use of resources, important as that is, and more with improving the quality of health care provided the aged. A growing school of thought holds that many of the aged would be better served by less aggressive treatment. As the human body begins to disintegrate, heroic forms of medical intervention, such as radical surgery for metastasized cancer, may add weeks or even months to a patient's life. Has the patient been informed of the risks and benefits and has he consented to treatment that may extend his life only at the cost of paralysis and pain? The growth of "living wills" indicates that an increasing number of individuals have opted against prolonging their lives for a short while at the cost of undergoing radical surgery and painful convalescence.

The need for health services across the entire age spectrum is often commingled with the need for various types of social services, but nowhere is this more striking than in the case of older persons in failing health. Many families who have been worn down emotionally, physically, or financially welcome the opportunity to institutionalize an older relative for whom they have been caring. Many persons in nursing homes, old age homes, and mental institutions belong to families that are no longer able or willing to cope with them.

The challenge to society is not to build more long-term facilities to which such patients can be transferred. Rather, we should encourage community experimentation in providing older persons with the range of basic health and other services they need, preferably in their family settings.

These brief considerations point to important actions that can improve health care without waiting for the introduction of a comprehensive system of national health insurance. Let us state again that NHI would not assure that these or other current needs would be met. The several cases under review underscore that many gains in access to and improvement in the quality of health care do not require large new expenditures or more physicians, but involve improved coordination among health and related resources.

We have looked at health reforms by inspecting the major proposals before Congress and by delineating possible solutions to the problems of four underserved groups. We will now explore a third approach involving priority recommendations directed at each of the four dimensions of health reform—access, quality, cost containment, and equity. This third approach will also consider the interrelations among these proposals so that we can identify optimal solutions.

With respect to access, we must note again that during the last decade there have been significant gains in providing critical health care services for hitherto underserved groups. But our earlier discussion identified continuing shortcomings in access, especially for primary care, among many low-income families; the desirability of providing dental services for their children; the need of older persons for improved access to long-term care. Improved access, then, lies more at the periphery than at the center of health reform, since dental care and long-term care for the aged represent the remaining principal challenges.

However the issue of improved access is assessed, need exists for improvements in quality to which access is linked in ambulatory care and in institutional care.

The basic dilemma of all efforts at quality assurance derives from the need to rely on physicians themselves to monitor the quality of care. With regard to improving the quality of ambulatory care, the following approaches appear promising. The single most important way for a physician to stay abreast of changes in medical knowledge and technology is to have a hospital appointment, especially in a hospital with a strong teaching program. A study of "Physicians' Staff Appointments in Southern New York" (1974), based on data for the late 1960s, revealed that approximately 15 percent of all physicians involved in direct patient care did not have hospital staff appointments; the highest proportions without hospital appointments were among the younger and older members, women, foreign medical graduates, and those who practiced in the low-income areas of the city.[54] A priority challenge to the emerging planning structure (Health Services Agency) should be to explore how the number of physicians without hospital appointments could be reduced; to consider how additional types of refresher training opportunities might be instituted to meet the needs of these practitioners; to determine whether a system of consultants involving the leadership of the medical profession could be instituted to review the level of care provided in publicly supported clinics.

With regard to improving the quality of hospital care, it would probably be wise to monitor the growing experience with PSROs. It is not clear that the gains will justify the effort. At the least, current developments should be closely observed with an aim of determining whether they make a significant contribution to improved quality.

An alternative approach to monitoring the quality of hospital care would be the routine collection by an authorized agency of basic data about admissions, treatments, and discharges that would be reviewed to identify institutions with apparently aberrant patterns—for example, a disproportionately high rate of elective operative procedures such as hysterectomies. As questionable practices are identified, consultants could visit these hospitals to determine the reasons for the deviations and, if they were grounded in poor practices, remedial action would be instituted.

The current efforts underway in New York and several other states to establish minimum acceptable levels of utilization for specialized services should also improve the quality of hospital care.

If the Health Services Agencies can improve linkages among hospitals in their areas in order to facilitate the flow of patients requiring complex care to the major centers, a gain in quality could be achieved.

Similarly, it would be desirable for the HSAs to link nursing homes to nearby teaching hospitals so that the hospitals could assume responsibility for assessing the changing medical needs of nursing home patients; provide hospital care when indicated; make arrangements for follow-up care after the patient is returned to the nursing home. The better nursing homes have such affiliations. The challenge to the HSAs is to see that all nursing homes establish effective linkages.

The foregoing recommendations with respect to improved access and higher quality do not imply vast increases in health care expenditures, at least not if caution is exercised in expanding entitlements to dental and long-term care. The vast cost escalation that has taken place over the past decade, inflation aside, stems from the substantial increase in health resources—physicians, hospital beds, new services—and the full cost reimbursement mechanisms that removed the conventional constraints on most providers to keep their expenditures down.

A serious effort at cost containment therefore must address both of these issues: the increase in resources and methods for reimbursing providers.

With respect to the former, since physicians generate large incremental expenditures in the health care system, estimated earlier to be in the $250,000 range per physician per year, further expansion of their numbers should be discouraged in favor of the training and deployment of physician extenders and nurse-practitioners.

Inasmuch as hospital care accounts for about one-third of the total costs of health care, cost containment must focus on controlling bed capacity. The nation has taken the first steps via certificate-of-need legislation to slow the increase in bed capacity, but thus far only a few proposals for expansion have been denied. However, it often takes a considerable period of time before a newly installed mechanism begins to operate effectively. We cannot assume that this approach has failed any more than we can be sanguine about its future success.

Limiting new hospital capacity is important, but equally important is the elimination of excess beds and duplicated services. Significant economies will be realized not through reduced utilization, which is the basic approach of the PSRO, but only through the permanent elimination (or conversion) of surplus institutions. Real savings are made when entire hospitals are closed. Their elimination, however, is difficult to effect because of pressures from physicians who will lose their staff appointments, hospital workers who will become unemployed, and members of the community who will have to seek treatment elsewhere.

Serious and sustained efforts at closing surplus institutions are a major challenge to the newly created Health Services Agencies which they must address. Alternative staff appointments must be offered to qualified physicians; excess employees should be eligible for priority hiring at other health facilities; they should also have access to retraining and be provided with appropriate separation allowances. For the community, alternative treatment facilities must be identified and their ability to assume the additional patient load assessed and, if necessary, reinforced. Community leaders must be consulted early and persuaded of the logic of closing the facility so that they can help to moderate the inevitable public opposition.

Several attempts to control the proliferation of expensive duplicated services have also been initiated. The federal government is limiting highly specialized therapeutic centers on a regional basis in its End-Stage Renal Program; some state agencies are authorizing reimbursements only to facilities that meet stipulated utilization levels; Blue Cross is increasingly using its reimbursement powers to prevent hospitals from

opening expensive new services in areas where adequate capacity exists. As with certificate-of-need legislation, it would
be premature to judge the efficacy of these methods for significant cost control.

Detailed Medicare experience by state and region is providing a wealth of management information, which should be
explored for cost control purposes. These data demonstrate
that the average hospital stay in the Northeast is 50 percent
longer than in the West; that the proportion of hospital admissions involving surgery in the Northeast (35 percent) is substantially higher than in the South (25 percent).[32] It is difficult
to conceive of a combination of demographic, income, and
cultural factors that would justify such wide differentials.
Much of the explanation must lie in professional practice.
These findings clearly warrant further study. If it is learned
that the outcomes of alternative treatment modalities are approximately the same, then it behooves third-party reimbursers
to convince providers in the high cost areas to adopt practices
followed in low cost areas. This will entail a difficult educational campaign but one with potentially high return.

The foregoing is a suggestive, rather than an exhaustive,
identification of methods whereby reducing the inflow of resources into the health care system would help moderate rapid
cost escalation. Our second approach addresses possible reforms of reimbursement mechanisms.

The current literature in medical economics is replete with
proposals aimed at showing cost acceleration engendered by
the practice of expenditure-based reimbursement. Much of
this literature is disingenuous, since it fails to acknowledge
that we lack a model for the noncompetitive sector. Analysis
has shown that the so-called incentive reimbursement contracts of the Department of Defense are more nearly pro-
paganda instruments than effective methodology. And the

history of public utility rate-setting is not encouraging, even in states that have innovative rate commissions. The principle is irrefutable: if an economic unit provides a service that the public wants and needs, it can continue to provide such a service over time only if its revenues equal or exceed its outlays, including a return on capital.

There is every reason for third-party payors and hospital rate commissions to continue to experiment with approaches aimed at containing the rise in hospital costs. If the authorities keep a tight lid on reimbursements, these institutions may have no alternative but to invade their endowments, skimp on their depreciation, and eliminate all optional services. But once these adjustments have been made, the institution would be mired in poverty.

Economists believe that improved organization and better management offer potential responses to a tight reimbursement policy. But since no one group or individual—not the administrator, the trustees, or the medical staff—effectively controls the hospital, there is no mechanism to assure that improved operations will be the answer to financial hardship. Overzealous third-party payors and rate commissioners run the risk of sapping the industry of its vitality.

From society's point of view, the objective should be to shrink the overexpanded hospital system back to required size, to eliminate expensive duplicated services, to encourage ambulatory care and nursing homes as less expensive alternatives to hospital inpatient treatment. At the same time experiments to improve reimbursement mechanisms should continue. But care must be taken not to force the entire industry into a state of poverty precluding innovation.

The difficulty with this prescription is the absence of adequate social machinery with which to accomplish these complex goals, even if consensus were reached that they should be pursued. However, some of the components have been put into place, and we are now beginning to learn to use them. Certainly the complex objective of economizing in the provision of hospital care by exercising tight controls over capacity and services will be difficult to accomplish, and new and improved machinery will be required. Current discussions about incentive budgeting indicate that some health planners are aware of the industry's need to continue to accumulate capital. If hospitals break even at a point that barely covers their depreciation and if they are not permitted to accumulate any surplus, our society will have inadvertently blocked the path of future medical progress.

This brings us to the third aspect of cost containment, which involves recommendations aimed at improving the health of the American people by linking the health care system more effectively with other social systems. Earlier, we referred to the payment of transportation costs so that indigent rural patients could get to neighboring health facilities; to the strengthening of school health services; to the loneliness of the aged, which suggests greater social participation as an alternative to more health services. Elsewhere we have called attention to the importance of the Food Stamp Program for improving the health of the poor.

There is much interaction between health services and other social systems, some of which is broadly recognized, other less appreciated. The reduction of the speed limit on the nation's highways, which was adopted as an oil conservation measure, turned out to have important life-saving consequences. Compared to Western Europe, the United States has excessively high homicide rates, heavily concentrated among adolescents and young adults. If the high youth unemployment, especially among the alienated low-income minorities, were reduced, we might reasonably expect a significant reduction in their excessively high mortality. High pregnancy rates among unmarried teenage girls are currently recognized to be a serious public health challenge. Without minimizing the importance of providing these adolescents with access to adequate health care services, we can state that the root of their difficulties lies elsewhere—in broken families, in poor schools, in social maladjustment.

Many believe that the ultimate solution to our rising health costs is health education. This is a worthy proposal, but it does not provide an answer to our disappointing record with respect to smoking, overeating, alcohol, lack of exercise—subjects on which the American people have been well informed.

There are strong reasons to encourage greater efforts at health education. A "Spock for older persons" might enable our aged to bear their infirmities better by understanding that medical science has little to offer them, but that old age is not so overwhelming when they remember Churchill's quip: "What's the alternative."

This brings us to the last dimension of health reform, the goal of greater equity. If the objectives of improved access for the rural poor, the urban poor, children, and older persons to existing and new health care services as outlined above were achieved, and if progress with respect to quality assurance in ambulatory, hospital, and nursing home care could be speeded up, a significant gain in equity would be achieved.

A major challenge is the reform of Medicaid, which at present consists of fifty-four different federal-state and -territorial programs. The first priority should be to broaden eligibility, which currently is categorically determined; thus, individuals not eligible under Social Security or Aid for Dependent Children or Supplemental Security Income may not be currently eligible for Medicaid even though their need (poverty status) is as great as that of the eligibles.

There are also gross differences in the income standards for eligibility (for a family of four), from under $2,500 in Texas to over $4,500 in several of the large northern states. Moreover, eighteen states do not provide any coverage except for persons on welfare, while the remainder recognize "medical indigency" but use limits ranging from $2,200 in Tennessee to $5,300 in Wisconsin.[30]

These gross differences are also reflected in wide differentials in average annual expenditures per recipient: U.S. average expenses for 1973 for an aged patient amounted to $912, with a low of $178 for West Virginia and a high of $2,419 for Connecticut.[30]

At present, Medicaid covers the costs of health services for only about 60 percent of the poor, if we use the federal standard of poverty. Eight states cover less than one out of five of their poor; only six cover 90 percent.

Between 1970 and 1976, the number of Medicaid recipients increased by about three-fifths. The major increase occurred among children under twenty-one, who constitute almost half of the 23 million enrollees. Currently, the medically indigent (that is, those not on welfare) comprise 21 percent of all enrollees and account for 43 percent of all Medicaid expenditures.

Any serious effort to improve equity in health care must address the reform of Medicaid. Embedded as Medicaid is in the welfare system, it does not now have the flexibility to assist a great many poor people who are not on the welfare rolls. The federal government must increase the flexibility of Medicaid to cover the large numbers of poor not now covered, and, at the same time, it must assure that the mandated minimum services are in fact available to all who are eligible. It has been argued that Medicaid cannot be reformed until the welfare system is reformed. Others argue that the reform of Medicaid is an essential concomitant of any reform of the welfare system.

Since the Carter Administration is committed to addressing both welfare reform and national health insurance, some progress toward greater equity in the provision of health care is a necessary and desirable first step. Such a step would give the country additional time to decide between introducing catastrophic health insurance or comprehensive national health insurance.

We have now presented three contrasting approaches to health reform: a critical review of current Congressional proposals; an analysis of the priority needs of underserved groups; and the next steps to improved access, quality, cost containment, and equity. The answer that has emerged is that considerable progress can be made on each of these four fronts without producing an untenable strain on the federal budget and without threatening to stifle progress in the delivery of medical care services.

Our health care system has operated with reasonable effectiveness, especially when compared with other essential public services, such as education, welfare, and the criminal justice system. Every social system, including health care, requires continual surveillance so that its shortcomings can be identified and efforts made to reduce and eliminate them. However, social intervention is difficult and costly. To avoid frustration, the level of public expenditures must be determined by what is feasible in terms of existing knowledge and potential resources. Health reform is essential. But health reform is a commitment, a process, not a one-time action. In our concluding chapter, the nature of this process within the framework of American democracy is assessed.

12

Health Reform in a Democracy

WE HAVE CONSIDERED the process of health reform in the United States in terms of goals and mechanisms. Now we will stand back to consider the role of health reform in the context of the democratic society within which it must be accomplished. We will first reconsider our list of priority reforms that appear to command considerable approval and then identify the forces and institutions that might prevent our effecting these desirable changes. The third step will be to consider the institutions that are basic to our democratic system and to assess their ability to further priority health reforms.

We have seen that a considerable number of Americans living in sparse or heavily populated areas find it difficult to obtain access to needed health services. The principal societal impediments to access are the lack of providers—particularly physicians, hospitals, or specialized services—and the paucity of the individual's personal or family resources in the form of income, insurance, or Medicaid benefits. Of course, there are differing estimates of the actual numbers of people without access to medical help, and as many reasons for them. But most analysts agree that improved access to health services should be included on a priority list.

It is more complicated to limn the concept of quality. Despite differences of definition and criteria of assessment, a disturbingly large number of persons suffer dysfunctional consequences as a result of questionable drug therapy or surgical interventions. The subject of quality surely belongs on the nation's health agenda. But it is debatable whether there are governmental measures that can significantly improve the quality of existing medical services.

Only a few sophisticated economists question the concern with costs. They know that health costs have moved up steeply and give no evidence of leveling off. But they do not consider it amiss that the American public will devote even as much as 10 or 12 percent of their GNP to health care. However, most Americans are disturbed when their physician charges $50 or $75 for a first visit; that one day in the hospital, with few special services, may result in a bill of $350 or even $500.

Many individuals concerned with health costs, from senior officials in the federal government to the managers of local Blue Cross Plans, are disturbed by the accelerating costs and believe that the financial underpinnings of the health care system depend on an early leveling off of these costs.

There is a broad consensus that all individuals are entitled to approximately the same range and quality of life-preserving and life-extending health services, irrespective of differences in their income, status, race, age, or residence. Accordingly, the equity issue is included in most lists concerned with priorities in health reform.

The principal targets, then, for health reform in our democracy include:

—Expanded access to health care for the underserved.
—Improved quality of health services throughout the country.
—A leveling off in cost escalation of health services.
—Equity in health care for all groups of the population.

To enable the reader to understand the forces that block our achievement of these priority objectives, we will outline briefly some of the realities of contemporary American society. Successful reforms ensue only when sufficient and sustained leverage has been applied to existing institutions and power centers to force them to respond. The only alternative is for society to allocate new resources to establish new institutions to provide desired services. As we shall see, there are barriers to each of these approaches.

Broadened access, improved quality, and greater equity in health care services depend on a mixture of additional resources and on their redistribution. Let us consider each in turn. First, with respect to additional resources: by the end of Fiscal Year 1977—that is, by September 30, 1977—total expenditures for health care in the United States will be in the range of $160 billion. Let us estimate that the eradication of serious barriers to access, modest improvements in quality, and some reasonable progress toward greater equity would conservatively require a net new investment of 25 percent, stretched over a three-to-five-year period. This would involve new expenditures, solely for meeting these priority goals, of about $60 billion if the recent cost escalation continues. We are talking, then, about additional resources of not less than $12 and up to $20 billion a year to correct a part of the current shortcomings. This calculation does not include any provision for broadening services.

Additional dollars alone cannot provide services for people who currently have limited access to physicians, hospitals, and other providers. A successful reform program would require at a minimum the building of new institutions, the relocation of health practitioners, the establishment of new services, the modification of community practices including the reduction of class and race discrimination.

None of the foregoing goals is impossible to achieve, but to accomplish one or more of them would be difficult. There is little in the record of the last quarter century to suggest that the substantial differences in quality between health care available in a low-income rural community and that available to a high-income suburban area have narrowed. Similarly, although we know that Medicare and Medicaid contributed substantially to narrowing the gap in access to medical care among groups differentiated by income, education, and race, only an optimist would claim that we have made significant gains on the equity front. Some gain, yes; significant gains, no.

Progress toward cost containment appears to conflict with efforts to improve access, quality, and equity. Some would deny this by claiming that a radically new system of organizing and paying for health care, through a federalized system of national health insurance with coverage for the entire citizenry, would permit gains on all of the above fronts and at the same time force a lid on total expenditures.

A few points in rebuttal. It is possible, but by no means certain, that Congress could succeed in capping health expenditures or at least slowing the rate of increase. But in the absence of draconian new legislation that would prohibit the public from increasing its personal expenditures for health care, a reasonable forecast must anticipate increased total outlays. In a society marked by substantial differentials in income and wealth, such a prospect must be assumed.

Equally remote is the process whereby the current supply of health facilities and personnel would be redistributed to assure greater equity between the more and less favored regions of the country, and between areas within the same region that have substantially differing access to health services. No democracy that has undertaken even major reforms has succeeded in substantially narrowing these differences. Moreover, the record of regional redistribution in communist societies is not much better.

This summary review of priority health goals and the identification of impediments to their early achievement bring us to the heart of this chapter: to place the issue of health reform alongside the institutions of a democratic society in order to explore their congruence and dissonance. Such an analysis must consider the processes of securing consensus, the mechanisms for implementing reforms, and the resource flows required to maintain the new structure.

With respect to the processes for obtaining consensus, we will begin with the issue of the present distribution of power in the health care industry and the likelihood of obtaining agreement among the major parties for major reforms such as national health insurance. A first step is to recognize the multiple power centers: first, the organized medical profession, including the medical school and research community (the Association of American Medical Colleges) and private practitioners (the American Medical Association), many of whose interests run parallel but who differ from time to time on specific issues. Both organizations would oppose reforms restricting the degree of freedom that physicians now enjoy to determine their fields of specialization and the location of their practices. To simplify the discussion, we will ignore other powerful groups of health personnel, such as dentists and nurses, each of which is well organized to achieve its separate and distinct goals.

The second power center comprises the large insurance organizations, particularly the Blue Cross Plans and the profit-making companies selling individual and group policies. These are large and powerful organizations with operating budgets of over $7.3 billion annually, with clients in every state and in a great many localities, with large payrolls that provide employment for many and career opportunities for some. Although some commercial companies imply that they do not make money from selling health insurance, the fact that the larger companies continue to sell such insurance reduces the credibility of their claim, especially since selling health policies is often linked to selling life, accident, and annuity policies, which we know is profitable.

The third large power center consists of the nation's hospitals, particularly our short-term general hospitals that do not operate for profit and that constitute the principal health facility in most communities. There are over 5,000 community hospitals, and their boards are customarily drawn from among the community's elite in terms of status, power, money. In many places, large or small, the hospital, more than any other local institution, is the focal center around which different groups rally.

The last important power center involves the highly diversified participants that are involved in profit-making activities in the health industry, from the large pharmaceutical companies to the small nursing home operator. These enterprises are heavily or solely dependent on producing and selling to various purchasers, including hospitals, physicians, government, and the consumer. In light of the rapid expansion of the health care area, we can assume that most of these enterprises enjoy a reasonable rate of profits. Consequently, each is more likely to opt for the continuation of the present system than to join those who advocate major reforms. Physicians continue to be high earners. Many are restive about the growing amount of paperwork they must attend to, particularly if they treat a large number of Medicare or Medicaid patients. This and related experiences, such as governmental pressure to justify their treatment plans, make them wary about reforms that are likely to enlarge the responsibilities of the bureaucracy. They have little to gain and much to lose from a major restructuring of the health care system.

The insurance companies, especially the commercial companies, know that the more radical proposals in the Congressional hopper, such as the Kennedy-Corman bill, provide little or no future role for them in the selling and administration of prepayment plans. No business enterprise can view with equanimity prospective legislation that will force it to withdraw from a market in which it has operated for years and for the most part profitably.

The community general hospitals are in a somewhat different position, since many of them are currently finding it difficult to stay financially afloat. They recognize the mounting efforts of governments to contain the upward spiral of hospital costs, and they are increasingly constricted by new rules and regulations limiting their freedom of action in many directions. Some among the hospital leadership see possible gains from a system of national health insurance, since they assume that the federal government will provide the sums required to keep the nation's hospital plant functioning effectively. But to date, most of the hospital leadership has been uneasy about a heavy prospective involvement of the federal government and favors more modest reforms aimed at providing hospital insurance for the entire population.

As noted above, the commercial suppliers of goods and services to health providers and consumers have no reason to favor large-scale reform. They have felt the heavy hand of government in the ever tighter rules and regulations limiting their freedom of action to introduce new products without elaborate testing, and they see only difficulties and dangers from reforms that would enlarge the role of government in health care.

This first inspection suggests that the principal power centers see little gain and substantial losses from major reforms of the health care industry. The question arises, therefore: Who are the protagonists of the health reform that has won the guarded approval of the Democratic Party and President Carter? The answer is: A loose association of concerned consumers, of labor union leaders (whose members indirectly and sometimes directly must cover steeply rising insurance premiums), some political leaders who see health reform as a winning issue, and many health analysts in academic and governmental positions who believe that the present system is both inefficient and inequitable and could be substantially improved. Our concern is less in estimating the relative strength of the contesting parties and more in reviewing the manner in which our democracy deals with such emerging challenges and the decision-making processes on which it relies.

Ours is a system of challenge and response. Congressmen are likely to enact radically new proposals only when there are clear and unmistakable signals from their constituents that nonaction is the greater risk. For example, when Congress was thoroughly annoyed with the arrogance of the monopolies in 1890, it passed the Sherman Anti-Trust Act. The banking difficulties of 1907 led to the Aldrich Commission and the passage of the Federal Reserve Act in 1913; the collapse of the market system in the Great Depression of 1930–33 paved the way for the New Deal legislation of 1933–35. This is the way our democracy operates.

If the American people become unable or unwilling to meet the steeply rising insurance premiums for health care; if a growing number of community hospitals are forced to close because the funds they receive from third-party reimbursement do not cover their operating expenses; if the costs of Medicaid to the federal and state governments get so high that legislators must reduce benefits to a point where the poor can no longer obtain basic health services—then, but probably only then, would the stage be set for major health reform. At that point many of the presently silent and unengaged public, who now prefer to leave matters alone, could be recruited to the side of the reformers.

The foregoing analysis could be called tendentious because it gives short shrift to present shortcomings that, in the view of many informed critics, long ago reached serious proportions: steeply escalating and still rising costs; severe budget pressures on federal, state, and local governments; insufficient and inadequate care; multiple inequities, including the public's underwriting the expensive training of physicians without extracting any service from them in return. We need not challenge this list of complaints to argue that it has not lowered the resistance to major reform from the principal interest groups.

Sometimes a society can undertake substantial, even fundamental, reforms without a shift in power relations among the key interest groups, especially if it is in a position to invest substantial new resources. This was the situation in the mid-1960s, when the Johnson Administration bought off the continuing opposition of the American Medical Association to Medicare by promising that, in establishing the new system, it would protect the traditional pattern of patient-doctor relations.

The Medicare negotiations led to a significant reform without undue disturbance of the existing system. The liberals urged acceptance of the "deal" in the belief that time would lead to further and more radical changes; in their view, national health insurance was not far behind. Conservatives, realizing that Medicare was likely to pass in any event, bargained for what they could get, in the hope and expectation that, with more time, they could regroup to thwart future reforms.

So much for the process of gaining political consensus, the foundation for any significant change in a democratic society. The second challenge involves consideration of how significant changes can be achieved within the basic values and institutions that continue to command the respect and approval of the citizenry and that they are reluctant to modify and unwilling to cast aside.

Ours is a federal system of government that reserves wide powers to the states, which in turn are able to delegate them to local government. The first consequence of this federalized system is the modest role that the federal government plays in the delivery of direct services on a day-to-day basis to the population. With the exception of the mail, the federal government does not directly interact with the citizenry. Police, sanitation, fire, education, transport, welfare, employment, training, and many more services for the public are provided primarily under the aegis of state and/or local government, with no direct participation of the federal government beyond occasional financing.

The degree to which the federal government can alter the quantity and quality of health care provided the average citizen depends, therefore, on the capacity and capability for change of state and local governments. The only alternative would be if the federal government were to bypass state and local government and work through existing or newly established private or quasi-public instrumentalities. If the federal government were to commit itself to providing health services to the entire public—as distinct from undertaking to pay for such services—it would thereby assume the responsibility for organizing and delivering services, an arena in which it has had limited experience and in which the record is poor. It is one thing for the federal government to mail monthly Social Security checks to beneficiaries; it is quite another for it to implement a commitment to provide improved health care to all the American people.

The weakness of many state and local governments is only one constraint. A related problem involves the difficulties of the federal government's commanding the human resources required to provide an acceptable level of health services. American society has long placed a high value on the individual's right to determine for himself where he lives and works, and consequently, many communities are unable to attract and retain critical health manpower. Although the federal government has recently enacted new legislation aimed at assigning young physicians and other health professionals to underserved areas in return for the financial assistance provided them during their training, it remains to be seen how well the new carrot-and-stick approach will work. It runs counter to our tradition to require needy young men and women to undergo a period of indentured service. Moreover, one may wonder about the quality of care that is likely to be provided by individuals who resent serving at the will of legislators and impatiently await the time when they can relocate.

A further issue involves quality assurance. There is little point to the federal government's assuming a commitment to provide health services to the entire population unless it is able to build in some mechanism for monitoring both the quantity and particularly the quality of services. However, accountability and quality control are difficult to design and implement, even in such simple services as basic education or criminal justice. The problems are many times greater in the case of medical care, which involves considerations of responsibility, judgment, and compassion, as well as technical competence.

We assume that professional behavior must be controlled by professionals. However, the recent steep rise in malpractice litigation can be explained at least in part by the failure of the medical profession to police itself effectively. It remains to be seen whether the PSRO effort, based on nurses or residents reviewing patient records, will be more than perfunctory. It may contribute modestly to cost containment, which was the principal objective of the sponsor of the legislation (Senator Bennett of Utah), but whether it will contribute to quality assurance remains in doubt.

At the heart of the difficulty with quality assurance is the social dilemma posed by the reluctance of professionals to police themselves and the limited ability of nonprofessionals to discharge that responsibility effectively. If the system of control depends on law, rules, and regulations, and nonprofessionals are responsible for the results, it is likely that the assessments will be *pro forma* rather than substantive. The best prospect for quality assurance lies in the continued development of the profession's code of behavior. This approach may be excruciatingly slow, but it should be maintained until the proponents of an alternative system come forward with a practical plan.

The growing consensus in favor of greater equity in access to health care services directly conflicts with the persistence of gross differentials in income and wealth characteristic of the United States. The proponents of greater equity hold that individuals and families at opposite ends of the income scale should receive approximately the same quantity and quality of health services, despite the ability of the wealthy to command more attention and superior accommodations and to seek treatment from the most skilled practitioners. This contention is unrealistic. Great Britain has moved a long way to force the issue of equity, including the recent restrictions on beds for private patients in government hospitals, but only a naive observer of the British health scene believes that the slum dweller seen at the outpatient department of a large city hospital by a foreign medical graduate receives the same level of care as a member of the high-income group. As noted earlier, further inequities derive from gross differentials in the health resources that are available in different regions of the country.

We have called attention to several constraints, specifically the capacity of state and local governments to carry a larger share of responsibility in the delivery of care; the disinclination of a democracy to interfere with the freedom of individuals to choose their places of residence and work; the necessity for a society to rely on professionals to control their own members; and finally, the incompatibility of a national commitment to provide a single acceptable level of care to all members of the society in the face of large income differentials.

This brings us to the last set of considerations that involve the conditions required to keep any system, new or old, conservative or radical, performing at an acceptable level of efficiency. The critical elements in the maintenance of every large social system are the flow of resources, sources of innovation, mechanisms for distributing available income among providers, and arrangements for social control.

The economists are not unrealistic in considering the market a unique mechanism for mediating resource allocation, innovation, distribution of income, and protection of the public. When competitive markets operate effectively, they make a major contribution—and at low cost—to achieving these critically important goals. But even fully competitive markets alone are not always responsive. In the case of medical care, additional social arrangements are required to assure the development of trained personnel, to provide access to essential services for people who lack purchasing power, to finance research, and otherwise to pick up the pieces that do not attract private investors.

One single statistic, the proportion of personal health expenditures that is met by the consumer directly—slightly over 35 percent—is proof that our contemporary health care system differs from that of a classic competitive model.[9] Although competition, in its classic guise, does not exist in the health care industry, the society cannot turn its back on the critical functions that a competitive market performs with respect to resource allocation, income distribution, innovation, and social control. Each must be considered and addressed.

With respect to the flow of resources, it is inevitable, no matter what system is in operation, that any steeply rising level of expenditures cannot be indefinitely sustained because of the scramble in the public arena over the allocation of scarce dollars among such important goals as defense, employment, welfare, education, and environmental protection. In addition, the resistance of consumers directly as well as through the collective bargaining mechanisms will forestall the efforts of the protagonists to preempt an ever larger part of total available funds for any single activity such as health insurance.

Although many reform proposals frequently attract support on the basis of prospective economies, the sad truth is that the putative savings are seldom realized. Accordingly, the principal mechanism by which a costly program is brought under control is the drying up of additional resources. At that point, expenditures tend to level off, even decline.

Once this dampening process sets in—and it is inevitable—the fight over the distribution of the health dollar, previously obscured by the substantial increases in total resources, must become both more overt and more intense. The several organized interest groups, professionals and nonprofessionals alike, will use their power and influence at every level where decisions are made in order to protect their relative position. No organized group can afford to stay out of the fray.

A second likely consequence of a tightening financial situation will be reduced opportunities for actions aimed at narrowing differentials in access and narrowing the gap between regions with scarce resources. Each of the foregoing would require substantial new resources that by definition cannot be marshalled under conditions of financial stringency.

The opportunity to finance innovations in research, education, alternative delivery systems, and improved monitoring and evaluation is risked when the scramble for resources is intensified. The present always has the edge over the future. In an open-ended system in which the demand for services can never be fully met, those who must respond to voters are under pressure not to cut back on current programs in order to support innovations.

Although there are many drawbacks to the loosely articulated health care system that characterizes the United States in 1977, we must not overlook some tangential advantages that derive from multiple sources of financing. A strongly centralized system with a single source of financing is much less likely in periods of stringency to make funds available for innovations.

There is a growing consensus that no one group of professionals should be permitted to determine the conditions under which they work or the rewards to which they are entitled. But we cannot deduce from this principle that under a centralized or nationalized system decision-making by government officials about an important social service such as health care will lead to improved social outcomes. Consider the National Health Service in Great Britain as a case in point. Thirty years after it was established, health professionals, particularly physicians, have critical decision-making roles. This implies that while a profession may have greater or lesser freedom to shape the conditions under which it works, its influence remains substantial. There may be grounds for radically reorganizing our health care system, but it would be a mistake to assume that even far-reaching reform would transfer power from the hands of the profession to a group of elected or appointed officials more responsive to the public.

Our argument can be briefly summarized. The existing health care system in the United States has many defects, principally those characterizing access, quality, cost containment, and equity. Although the nation has been spending ever larger sums for health care, these expenditures have not eliminated the major shortcomings, partly because as performance is improved, expectations are adjusted upward.

Since additional money has not solved our problems, an increasing number of critics—convinced that the way in which the nation produces, distributes, and finances health care is responsible for most of the shortcomings—have focused attention on organizational changes. They advocate major reforms that eventually will lead to a national health system. But the political forces in opposition to nationalizing health care have the upper hand at present. Even if the proposal were enacted, the federal government would not be able to meet its commitments; it could do so only by riding roughshod over basic values and institutions. And even then, it would fall short of meeting its goals unless it were able and willing to invest more resources in health care. But it is just this increase that the reform is aimed to prevent.

If a radically new system were put into place and launched, troubles would inevitably develop. Conflicts would escalate

among providers for a larger share of the health dollar; poor
regions would present their claims for special consideration;
various groups would battle about the importance of conflicting goals.

The moral is clear. Health reform is as inevitable as it is
doomed to disappoint its advocates. The inevitability derives
from the fact that, in a dynamic society such as the United
States, with a population that is both increasing and relocat-
ing, with gains in real income, changes in life styles, and advances in science and technology, the health care system of
1980 must differ from that of 1940. Many innovations result
from changes occurring outside the political realm. An abbreviated list of changes includes the growth of health insurance,
the vastly accelerated flow of resources into the health care system, the specialization of American medicine, the building of
a health care system to support the needs of the burgeoning
suburban populations, and much more—including Medicare,
Medicaid, and expanded support for research.

Since many innovations and changes occurred without government's playing more than a modest role, what ground is
there for believing that a serious attempt to reform the health
care system under the aegis of the federal government is necessary or will prove constructive? There are four main reasons
for skepticism: three out of every five dollars spent on health
care still originate from outside the governmental arena; the
regional and area distribution of health resources is grossly un-
even; most members of the medical profession prefer to live
and work in large metropolitan communities; it will be difficult to assure future large inputs of new resources for the
health care system.

These realities should suffice as a warning that although
health reforms under governmental aegis may prove constructive, there is little prospect that any reform, even one well

designed and implemented, can meet the expectations of its proponents: to assure access for all, improve quality, contain costs, and establish a single level of care for all Americans.

An affluent democracy such as ours has the potentiality for using government to expand and improve the services available to its people. It has done so in the past and can do so again. But there is nothing in our experience with the delivery of critical services—in the areas of education, criminal justice, welfare—to suggest that, if the United States opts for a nationalized system of health care, the quantity and quality of the services made available to different groups, living in different parts of the country, would meet with broad citizen approval. The odds are overwhelming that the major improvements anticipated from health reform would not be forthcoming, unless the public were to concentrate most of its political energy and economic resources on this single goal. But that is just what a democracy, in its collective wisdom, is unlikely to do. The gains from such intense preoccupation with health reform— or any other fundamental reform—will not repay the efforts required. It is better for a nation to moderate its expectations, shape its goals to its resources, and follow a path where it can continue to learn from experience.

Additional Readings

The following few suggestions are directed to the nonspecialist reader who would like to explore a little further policy aspects of the contemporary health scene in the United States.

The recent collection of essays edited by John Knowles, M.D., *Doing Better and Feeling Worse: Health in the United States* (New York: W. W. Norton, 1977) offers at one and the same time the widest coverage of relevant themes and a challenge to much of the conventional wisdom. The fact that the authors include many leaders in the health care establishment makes the collection that much more pertinent.

Who Shall Live? by Victor Fuchs (Basic Books, 1974) is the best extant nontechnical treatment of critical health issues as viewed by an economist.

Why American medicine moved so strongly in the direction of specialization, which Congress is now committed to reversing, is set forth in a large authoritative work by Rosemary Stevens, *American Medicine and the Public Interest* (New Haven: Yale University Press, 1971), which has the added advantage of having been written by an author of British background.

The best volume on the alliances among health reformers, the leaders of academic medicine, and key members of Congress is Stephen P. Strickland's *Politics, Science, and Dread Disease* (Cambridge, Mass.: Harvard University Press, 1972), which recounts with much insight the growth of large-scale federal support for bio-medical research.

A sociologist's view of the influence of the social structure, politics, and medical science and technology upon the development of the health care system and the practice of medicine, which combines a conceptual framework with substantive research findings from here and abroad, is presented in David Mechanic's volume, *Politics, Medicine, and Social Science* (New York: Wiley-Interscience, 1974).

Ivan Illich's *Medical Nemesis: The Expropriation of Health* (New York: Pantheon, 1976) and Rick J. Carlson's *The End of Medicine* (New York: Wiley-Interscience, 1975) articulate the radical, antiestablishment position that has elicited heated controversy in recent years.

A useful introduction to the thorny issues of national health insurance is provided by Karen Davis's *National Health Insurance: Benefits, Costs and Consequences* (Washington, D.C.: Brookings Institution, 1975).

It can be profitably supplemented by William A. Glaser's *Paying the Doctor: Systems of Remuneration and Their Effects* (Baltimore, Md.: Johns Hopkins University Press, 1970), a comparative study drawing upon the experiences of diverse systems in Europe, the Middle East, and the Soviet bloc.

Health Care: Can There Be Equity? by Odin W. Anderson (New York: Wiley-Interscience, 1972) is a realistic appraisal of the systems in the United States, Sweden, and England.

Three recent governmental publications are illuminating both for what they include and for what they omit:

Forward Plan for Health FY 1978–82. DHEW/PHS August 1976.

Baselines for Setting Health Goals and Standards. DHEW (HRA 76–640), September 1976.

The Complex Puzzle of Rising Health Care Costs. Council on Wage and Price Stability. Executive Office of the President, December 1976.

Finally, the interested reader may want to explore one or more of my publications:

Men, Money and Medicine. New York: Columbia University Press, 1969.

Urban Health Services: The Case of New York, edited by Eli Ginzberg. New York: Columbia University Press, 1971.

Regionalization and Health Policy, edited by Eli Ginzberg. Washington, D.C.: Government Printing Office, forthcoming, 1977.

Health Manpower and Health Policy, forthcoming, 1978.

Notes

1. Our British cousins remind us now and again that there is an alternative to the Teutonic tradition that long ago captured the American scholarly world. The majority of qualified scholars in the United States believe that of all the work written during the past decade, the one that may yet have the most influence on health policy is A. L. Cochrane's 80-odd pages on *Effectiveness and Efficiency—Random Reflections on Health Services*. London: The Nuffield Provincial Hospitals Trust, 1972.

2. Abel-Smith, B. "Value for Money in Health Services." *Social Security Bulletin* 37; Fuchs, V. *Who Shall Live?* New York: Basic Books, 1974; Forbes, W. H. "Longevity and Medical Costs." *New England Journal of Medicine* 283; Lalonde, M. *A New Perspective on the Health of Canadians*. Ottawa: Information Canada, 1974.

3. Council on Wage and Price Stability. *The Complex Puzzle of Rising Health Costs: Can the Private Sector Fit It Together?* Washington, D.C.: Executive Office of the President, December 1976.

4. Keynes, J. M. *A Tract on Monetary Reform*. London: Macmillan and Co., 1923.

5. Hirshfield, D. S. *The Lost Reform*. Cambridge, Mass.: Harvard University Press, 1970.

6. President's Commission on the Health Needs of the Nation. *Building America's Health: A Report to the President*, vol. 1. Washington, D.C.; U.S. Government Printing Office, 1952.

7. Carnegie Council on Policy Studies in Higher Education. *Progress and Problems in Medical and Dental Education: Federal Support versus Federal Control*. San Francisco: Jossey-Bass Publishers, 1976.

8. U.S. Department of HEW, Public Health Service, National Institutes of Health, Bureau of Health Professions Education and Manpower Training. *Health Manpower Source Book*, 20, *Manpower Supply—Educational Statistics for Selected Health Occupations: 1968*. Public Health Service Publication No. 263, Section 20, 1969; U.S. Department of HEW, Public Health Service, Health Resources Administration, National Center for Health Statistics. *Health Resources Statistics: Health Manpower and Health Facilities, 1975*. Rockville, Maryland: 1976.

9. Gibson, R. M. and Mueller, M. S. "National Health Expenditures Fiscal Year 1976," *Social Security Bulletin* 40.

10. Committee on the Costs of Medical Care. *Medical Care for the American People*. Chicago: The University of Chicago Press, 1932.

11. U.S. Department of HEW, Public Health Service, National Institutes of Health. *Basic Data Relating to the National Institutes of Health*, 1975.

12. Rayack E. *Professional Power and American Medicine: The Economics of the American Medical Association*. Cleveland: The World Publishing Company, 1967.

13. Somers, H. M. and Somers, A. R. *Medicare and the Hospitals: Issues and Prospects*. Washington, D.C.: The Brookings Institution, 1967.

14. Institute of Medicine. *Costs of Education in the Health Professions: Report of a Study*, Parts I and II. Washington, D.C.: National Academy of Sciences, January 1974; U.S. Department of HEW, Bureau of Health Manpower. *Selected Information on Health Professions Schools: BHM Support by Program, FY 1965–75*. Report No. 76–51 (Revised), April 1976.

15. U.S. Department of HEW. *Papers on the National Health Guidelines: Baselines for Setting Health Goals and Standards*. DHEW Publication No. (HRA) 76-640, September 1976.

16. Center for Community Health Systems and Department of Pediatrics, Faculty of Medicine, Columbia University. *A Proposal to The Robert Wood Johnson Foundation for a Child Health Care Project*. October 1973. Unpublished.

17. deVise, P., "Chicago's Continuing Doctor Drain," Working Paper I. 24. Chicago Hospital Study, November 1975.

18. U.S. Department of HEW, National Center for Health Statistics. *Health in the United States, 1975, a Chartbook*. DHEW Pub. No. (HRA) 76–1233. Rockville, Md.: 1976.

19. *The Wall Street Journal*, April 19, 1977.

20. U.S. Department of HEW, Bureau of Quality Assurance. *Professional Standards Review Organizations: 1977 Fact Book* (Preliminary Draft), February 1977.

21. Wilson, R. W. and White, E. L. "Changes in Morbidity, Disability, and Utilization Differentials Between the Poor and the Non-Poor: Data from the Health Interview Survey: 1964 and 1973." Paper presented at the 102nd Annual Meeting of the American Public Health Association, October 21, 1974.

22. *Source Book of Health Insurance Data 1976–77*. New York: Health Insurance Institute, 1976.

23. Dorsey, L. L. "The Health Maintenance Organization Act of 1973 (PL 93–222) and Prepaid Group Practice Plans." *Medical Care* 13.

24. Heyssel, R. M. and Seidel, H. M. "The Johns Hopkins Experience in Columbia, Maryland." *New England Journal of Medicine* 295.

25. Comprehensive Health Manpower Training Act of 1971 (PL 92–157).

26. Enterline, P., Salter, V., McDonald, A. D. and McDonald, J. C. "The Distribution of Medical Services Before and After 'Free' Medical Care—The Quebec Experience." *New England Journal of Medicine* 289.

27. U.S. Department of HEW, National Center for Health Statistics. *Health Manpower: A County and Metropolitan Area Data Book, 1972–75*. DHEW Publication No. (HRA) 76–1234, 1976.

28. Aday, L. A. and Andersen, R. *Access to Medical Care*. Ann Arbor, Michigan: Health Administration Press, 1975.

29. Wildavsky, A. "Doing Better and Feeling Worse: The Political Pathology of Health Policy." *Daedalus*, Winter 1977.

30. New Coalition Task Force on Medicaid Reform and National Health Insurance. "Medicaid Reform Issues: A Presentation of Options and Recommendations." Washington, D.C., February 18, 1977, mimeographed.

31. American Association of Neurological Surgeons, Neurological Manpower Commission. *Neurological Manpower Report: Summary and Conclusions* (Preliminary Report), May 27, 1975.

32. Gornick, M. "Medicare Patients: Regional Differences in Length of Hospital Stays, 1969–71." *Social Security Bulletin* 38.

33. Flexner, A. *Medical Education in the United States and Canada, A Report to the Carnegie Foundation for the Advancement of Teaching.* Carnegie Foundation Bulletin No. 4, New York, 1910.

34. Stevens, R. and Vermeulen, J. *Foreign-Trained Physicians and American Medicine.* DHEW Publication No. (NIH) 73–325. Washington, D.C., June 1972.

35. Gibson, G. "Emergency Medical Services," in E. Ginzberg, ed., *Regionalization and Health Policy.* Washington, D.C.: Government Printing Office, 1977 (in press).

36. *Economic Report of the President, January 1976.* Washington, D.C.: United States Government Printing Office, 1976.

37. U.S. Bureau of the Census. *Statistical Abstract of the United States: 1975,* 96th edition. Washington, D.C., 1975.

38. Fuchs, V. R. *Who Shall Live?* New York: Basic Books, 1974.

39. Feldstein, M. and Taylor, A. *The Rapid Rise of Hospital Costs.* Harvard Institute of Economic Research, Discussion Paper No. 531, Harvard University, Cambridge, Mass., January 1977.

40. The Congress of the United States, Congressional Budget Office. *Budget Options for Fiscal Year 1977,* March 15, 1976.

41. Mitchell, B. M. and Schwartz, W. B. "The Financing of National Health Insurance." *Science* 192.

42. U.S. House of Representatives, Subcommittee on Oversight of the Committee on Ways and Means. *Reports on Administration by the Social Security Administration of the End-Stage Renal Disease Program Established by Public Law 92–603 and on the Social Security Medicare Research Studies,* October 22, 1975.

43. Crossman, R. *Diary of a Cabinet Minister.* New York: Holt, Rhinehart and Winston, 1976.

44. Institute of Medicine. *Controlling the Supply of Hospital Beds.* Washington, D.C.: National Academy of Sciences, October 1976.

45. U.S. Department of HEW, Public Health Service. *Forward Plan For Health FY 1978–82.* Washington, D.C.: U.S. Government Printing Office, August 1976.

46. Hayflick, L. "The Cell Biology of Human Aging." *New England Journal of Medicine* 295.

47. Executive Office of the President: Office of Management and Budget. *Social Indicators 1973.* Washington, D.C.: U.S. Government Printing Office, 1973.

48. The Congress of the United States, Congressional Budget Office. *Five-Year Budget Projections: Fiscal Years 1978–1982,* December 1, 1976.

49. McLachlan, G. "The British Experience," in Ginzberg, E., ed., *Regionalization and Health Policy*. Washington, D.C.: U.S. Government Printing Office, 1977 (in press).

50. Pauly, M. and Redisch, M. "The Not-for-Profit Hospital as a Physicians' Cooperative." *American Economic Review* 63.

51. The Congress of the United States, Congressional Budget Office. *Catastrophic Health Insurance*. Washington, D.C.: U.S. Government Printing Office, January 1977.

52. The Congress of the United States, Congressional Budget Office. *Long-Term Care for the Elderly and Disabled*. Washington, D.C.: U.S. Government Printing Office, February 1977.

53. Brecher, C., Brudney, K., and Ostow, M. "The Implications of National Health Insurance for Ambulatory Care Services in New York City." *Bulletin of the N.Y. Academy of Medicine* 53.

54. Johnson, W., et al. *Physicians' Staff Appointments in Southern New York*. Health and Hospital Planning Council of Southern New York, 1974.

Index